"I am pleased to endorse and recommend Ryan's book, *Counterfeit Peace*. With great vulnerability Ryan captures what makes Rescue Mission ministry effective in helping the least of these find freedom in their lives.

I did not know Ryan before he encountered God's forgiveness and healing and knew him only slightly in his early years at Miracle Hill. The more I learned of him, the more I wanted to know as I saw his discipline, work ethic, and, more important, God working greatly within him.

When I led Miracle Hill, I often said, 'God has helped others through difficult times, and He can help you.' Some listened and were motivated to Seek God's help for themselves. In God's economy nothing is wasted, and Ryan's memories, while painful, provide much more hope than I could ever give to those struggling in impossible 'stuck' situations.

Ryan is a chosen servant, a talented, competent Christian leader and a careful steward of Miracle Hill's culture and Christ-centered focus. I am proud of his leadership, and I am grateful that Miracle Hill continues to reflect the call of Micah 6:8 to do justice, love mercy and kindness, and walk humbly before God."

—**Reid Lehman,** Past Miracle Hill President,
providing Governance consulting to rescue ministries
across the United States

"There is real transformation in Christ. We see it every day as we serve those struggling with alcohol and substance use disorders. Ryan's book is a stark testimony to this transformation. Jesus radically transforms all who come into a relationship with Him. Be encouraged and emboldened as you read this book and then share its many stories with those around you so they can be encouraged."

—**Gary W. Blackard,** President and CEO,
Adult & Teen Challenge USA.

"Life is a search. Whether it be meaning, purpose, or peace, we all desperately long for that which continuously eludes us. With vulnerability and authenticity, Ryan Duerk shares his own journey in discovering true peace after passionately pursuing the counterfeits. Whether you are searching for peace for yourself or know someone who is, *Counterfeit Peace* offers hope, direction, and a pathway to find freedom from the challenges and choices that keep you from experiencing the real thing. Ryan's story is one of many miracles that God has performed at Miracle Hill Ministries, and reading this book will open the door for you to receive your own miracle just like he did."

—**Tom De Vries,** President and CEO
Citygate Network

"Over the past few years, Ryan Duerk has emerged as leader among leaders in North America's city mission movement — which is amazing if you know his life story. He is someone who basically stumbled drunk through the front door of a mission and several years later walked out the back door with the keys in his pocket. In *Counterfeit Peace*, Ryan is raw and vulnerable, and divulges why the cracked and crooked path out of darkness and dependency must pass beneath the foot of the cross. If you have a wayward loved one who is struggling with addiction, this book will be an encouragement to you — and maybe to them — because it not only shows that no one is beyond hope, but it also clearly marks the way home."

—**John Ashmen,** Past President, Citygate Network
(The Association of Gospel Rescue Missions)

"I first met Ryan in his cleaned-out office as the Director for Overcomers. It was my first week as Lead Pastor of his home church and his last week in that position. I remember being compelled by his story that day and even more so now. Within these pages, you will not only read the captivating testimony of his life, but you will also discover how God uses that story to impact countless others as he now relentlessly leads the ministry that so thoroughly impacted him. I get the privilege to pastor men weekly who arrive at our church on the same vehicles Ryan did. You will learn why it is so easy for me to offer unshakeable hope that their story isn't over. Neither is yours. I pray that this account will provoke you to seek or offer the help my brother Ryan so passionately presents."

— **Travis Agnew,** Lead Pastor, Rocky Creek Church
Greenville, South Carolina

counterfeit
PEACE

RYAN DUERK

LUCIDBOOKS

To protect the privacy and dignity of people experiencing homelessness, addiction, despair, and death, names used in this book have been changed.

Dedicated to those who work tirelessly in rescue missions
each day, sitting in the dirt and sorrow and sharing
the love of Christ with the world, and to those in need
of hope who are stuck in the darkness of life.

May the place where your lives crash together
be filled with the grace of God.

The second is this: "You shall love your neighbor as yourself."
There is no other commandment greater than these.

—Mark 12:31

TABLE OF CONTENTS

INTRODUCTION

God. Is there any bigger word in existence? Sure, it looks small on the page—just three English characters on a page. But the implications of the word *God* are immeasurable in size and depth. If you try to define *God* as an idea, you face a limitless realm of possibilities. Is God big? How could God not be? Is God smart? What kind of stupid question is that? God is. . . infinite.

For me to tell you anything about who I am or the amazing journey the Lord has had me on, I have to preface my story and that of Miracle Hill with the idea that it all distinctly revolves around me trying to define that one little word. Over the years I attempted to fit God into a number of different boxes and failed. I tried to make Him fit my definitions and ideas, which always started and ended with me. Which is pretty small. Sure, I called God a whole lot of different things including expletives, but for a long time, it all came down to one specific point: I was "god" over my life, and no one—no one—was going to change that.

The stories you will read about my early life where I am miserable or lost or broken all share the reality that, in that moment, I was god over my own existence. You can see the problem. I was a terrible god. Many seasons of my life turned out terrible because as a god, I had zero power to change anything. The bottom line is that I am the worst god I have ever met, and I have met a lot. I broke everything that I was ever given. I burnt down every bridge I or someone else built. I took all the pretty things in my life and had a thorough time beating them and myself into the dirt.

I was untrustworthy and loathsome to be around, becoming a nightmare to many. I was a chameleon and would be whoever I had to be around whoever I happened to be around. I was a vampire, a parasite, and I bled everything and everyone who came around me dry. Point blank: I was an awful god; no one would have worshipped me. But worship myself, I did, which ultimately got me nowhere . . . but God.

I want to be honest with you for the duration that you happen to have this book in your hands. I want to tell you the truth that I have found in my existence without judgment, although I know that with transparency, judgment will come. Some things I will share won't be pretty or glorifying to anyone. This narrative is the best way I know to share how I struggled through this world and found my way from a life as my own god into the saving grace of God.

Now, you might want to put this book down because you think this is going to be just another story about Jesus, and you are sick of people telling you how great He is. Well, I don't want you to do that. What I want is for you to read and see how terrible I am, and then draw your own conclusions about Him.

A wise man once told me that for me to find out who God is, I would first have to find out who He isn't. That seemed like backward thinking at the time, but the consequences of that statement are great. You see, whenever we think we know best in our life and we leave all the decision-making to ourselves, we automatically assume the role of God in our life. We take out all the opportunity for something bigger than ourselves to manifest, and we go full bore into our own existence. We run around our life crashing into anything and everything that gets in our way. What if there is something bigger than us? What if there is a god or God out there that wants us to understand something, and we are just so blindly committed to doing it our way that we miss an opportunity? What if?

This memoir isn't the story of my whole life; rather it tells of the journey through my existence that led me to a specific place. There are many amazing people and stories that do not make it onto these pages. As I wrote the narrative, I was overwhelmed with how blessed my life has been even in the trials and storms. If I had written about every person, family member, or friend, *Counterfeit Peace* would have been ten times as long. Rather I tried to string together the stories that relate to the purpose of the book, my own personal crash course with the Creator.

Just keep reading. Some of this will be my story, but some of it will be about a larger story of grace in the world. It is overwhelmingly humbling that a sinner such as I would have an opportunity to share in any grace at all.

Prologue

2006

I came to in a haze unaware of what time it was or even what day it was. I was sitting on an old worn-out love seat on the back porch of the house I shared with a friend outside of Columbia, South Carolina. I looked to my right, located my pack of smokes, pulled one from the pack, lit the harsh menthol cigarette, inhaled, and began to look around. The sky appeared overcast, but the sun appeared low in the sky. Morning, or was it evening? They looked pretty much the same, so I quickly tried to piece together the last time I could remember being awake. I couldn't.

I made my way inside and went immediately to my stash. I threw back the pile of dirty clothes on the floor of my closet and revealed the box. I picked up the cardboard encased treasure and was immediately saddened by the weight of it. Empty, or nearly empty. Tearing open the cardboard, I pulled the sleeve out of the container seeing that all was not lost, there was about a glass left. Gripping the bag with one hand, and the other immediately going to the tap, I plunged the faucet into my mouth and began pulling the room temperature wine into my mouth, down my throat, and into my bile-filled empty stomach. As I squeezed the last drop into my mouth, my body started to fight the poison. Breathing deeply, I began to pace the living room, trying to keep the wine in my nutrient-deprived body. I succeeded.

Looking at the clock I realized it was four thirty in the afternoon. My roommate Coley would be home, if he came home, in about two hours. Having no money, barely any gas, and a screaming body, I made my way to the living room to determine how hard I could hit my current cash crop.

The DVDs stood against the wall. What was two or three hundred movies not six months ago, had dwindled down to thirty or so films. I scanned the titles—*Natural Born Killers*; all the *Lord of the Rings* movies; a variety of James Bond films, including my coveted *Casino Royale*; *Scarface*; my Tarantino collection; a few random X-Box games; and the pick of the litter, *Requiem of a Dream*. These were the titles that I was dreading to part with. I had been slowly selling my DVDs for a couple of months; first I took the movies that I cared the least about and then worked slowly inward toward my favorites. The movies and the ever-present alcohol were the only things that I considered friends at this point in my life. I snatched the DVDs up, grabbed my smokes, drenched myself with some Axe body spray, and headed out the door.

Movies were one of the many tools I used to escape. When my mind was racing about the destruction in my life, I would get drunk or high, and watch a movie. This would continue until I passed out and then I would do it again. Alone. There are weeks where the human voices from a screen were the only ones I heard.

The trip to the record store was uneventful other than worrying that I would run out of gas before I got any money. I didn't. I sold my lot, grabbed the forty dollars or so that the clerk gave, headed to the gas station, bought five dollars of gas and two packs of smokes, and then headed to Wal-Mart. Once inside the store I made a beeline to the wine section: $10.83 per box, Sunset Blush. I grabbed two and checked out. I immediately went back to the gas station, bought a large cup of ice water, went outside, poured the water out while keeping the ice in the cup, went to the trunk, snatched open the box, filled up my cup, and began to drive.

By the time that I got back to the house, it was six thirty or so, and I had evened out due to the wine I drank while driving. It is amazing how comparatively quiet the voices inside me would become after just a little bit of alcohol.

Coley was nowhere to be seen as I pulled in the driveway, and my anxiety, which was already being masked by the poison, subsided. I walked into the house with one box under my arm, my cup in my hand, and headed back to the porch. The sun was nearly down, and my body was exhausted. All I could think about was the wine and self-oblivion. My mind raced with the fact that I couldn't keep this up for much longer. I hadn't talked to a human being other than random cash register persons in weeks. Coley was completely ignoring me, and I desperately tried to make sure that he was either gone when I was home, or I was gone when he was home. My phone still worked, but I had quit answering it weeks ago. I would check my messages once a day if I had the courage, and every three days or so would call one of a couple of girls that I knew and cry on the phone with them for a half hour or so.

I didn't have any drugs at the time, but I had a large bag of stems and seeds from breaking down a bag of weed. I grabbed a handful of the rubbish and ground it down. I put the powdery organic material into a makeshift marijuana bowl, made of aluminum foil, and smoked the un-smokable and typically undesirable grounds. Stems have little THC in them, so the effect is minimal. As a bonus, the filterless device burned like fire. I knew I wouldn't get very high from it, but the ritual felt right, and the painful burn made me feel alive. The harsh smoke made me cough in between each pull from the pipe. Sometimes, the ritual alone makes you feel like you are accomplishing something. It can trick your brain into feeling high despite the absence of psychoactive substances. Regardless of content, a dull calm settled behind my eyes and added to the effect of the booze.

The porch I sat on had dirty, louvered windows and looked out on six or seven acres in the back yard. The first thing in my line of sight was a metal building that the property owner had previously used as a sawmill. The front of the building had a lean-to porch roof that was about twelve feet or so off the ground. I stared at the framing of the roof and imagined taking one of the lengths of rope in the yard and slinging it overhead. I would stick my head in a poorly made noose and swing. I wouldn't be found for days. I thought of this endlessly as the day became night and the roof slowly disappeared from my view with the setting sun. The ache in my stomach from lack of food was quieted by the sour sweet taste of the wine, the burn from the smoke, and the numbing nature of substance abuse. Coley never made it home, and sometime in the midevening, I passed out.

I woke up around eleven, and groped around in the dark until I found my lighter. I located my smokes, which had been smashed down in between the couch cushions, and as I lit my cigarette, I reached up and snatched the chain igniting the ceiling fan light. I located my cup and to my dismay, there was a small bug, maybe a fly floating in the drink. Apparently, he had drunk himself to death. I laugh nervously. I drank the rest of the cup and the fly, and I poured myself another round. As I sat back in my chair, I realized that the fly was retaliating against my disrespect. I reached the screen door seconds before the putrid pink; bile-filled liquid came screaming out of my body. I sat there kneeling in the grass attempting to breathe, as my body convulsed one dry heave after another.

Time is not a thing that I grasped well at this point in my life, but I felt like I dry heaved for a half hour. Once my body settled down, I went back inside, feeling much better, and poured myself another glass. I was a little annoyed that I had perhaps wasted a few ounces of alcohol by unintentionally watering the shrubs. This time I used ice to weaken the blow. I knew I needed food, so I moved to the kitchen but found nothing. I was stuck with just wine and did not have the energy to try to make it to a store. Also, I only had a few dollars left and didn't want to squander the cash on food.

I decided that a shower might perk me up, so I took my drink and my cigarette into the bathroom. I fired up the shower. I left all the lights off. Now most people might think this crazy, but I was completely capable of taking a shower with a full glass of wine while smoking an entire cigarette without getting it wet. I guess these types of things just come with practice in the life of an addict. After I tossed my smoke in the toilet, I took my normal showering position. I sat down on the floor with my knees pulled to my chest and let the scalding water pound my body until the heat started to weaken and I knew it was just moments from running out. It is amazing what the mind conjures up when you are drunk, malnourished, in the dark, and alone. My fear of forced sobriety from the water turning cold caused me to begrudgingly turn the shower off.

I got out and dried off with an overused sour towel. I dressed in the cleanest clothes that I could find and headed back to the porch. I drank, and then I drank some more, and then when that was done, I smoked. Then I drank, and I drank, and I drank.

I finally came to in the fog of the early morning sun. It was early enough to know that I had been out for some hours, and I was shaking. It was cooler on the porch than it had been the previous morning, and my body shook from the depth of my core, but it wasn't from the temperature. I looked around and located my smokes and my lighter. Lit one. Inhaled. Breathed out.

I went inside with the idea that I could warm up if I put a jacket on. I found my jacket crumpled up on the floor in front of the washing machine. I picked it up and started to put it on before realizing that it was filled with vomit. I threw it back down on the floor, went into my bedroom, found a hoodie, and put it on. I don't know when I vomited in the previous hours. That time was black to me. At this point over fifty percent of my time was in blackout. To this day, I don't remember years of my life.

Walking around, I attempted to locate the box of wine from the night before, but instead found a full box. I had drunk five liters of wine from one box and the first liter from the new box in the past twelve hours. Somewhere in the recesses of my mind, I understood why I was shaking. I poured myself some breakfast, downed the whole cup, watched as my shakes subsided visibly and in real time. Quickly my ever-present anxiety started to dissipate.

Let's talk about anxiety for a minute. Have you ever felt like you were trapped? Maybe as a kid when your siblings or friends locked you in a closet, you experienced the terror to which I am referring. Well, take that feeling and multiply it by thousands. Anxiety is like a fatal car crash where you are stuck in the car looking at bodies around you and watching the flames kick up. Imagine your heart feeling like it is going to pop right out of your chest, and your head swimming with so many thoughts all at once that it feels as if there are forty people in the room all talking at the same time. Couple that with a sense of foreboding and fear that few people ever get to experience outside of having a gun pressed against their head, and you are starting to grasp the anxious existence I had. This is the anxious existence of addiction. Although the anxiety is not based in reality, the addict who is stuck in the addiction cycle knows no form of escape outside of use. I believe that some people who have panic attacks know this feeling, but my anxiety was constant as the tide. The only answer to anxiety that I knew was booze or drugs. That's it. There was no other answer in my life.

I knew that there was a chance that Coley could come home to take a shower before going to work, and that scared me even more, so I made myself get dressed as if I was looking for a job. I changed into a wrinkled button-down shirt and a pair of dirty slacks and went to the bathroom.

Here was the evidence of vomiting from last night. Peppered all over the floor, toilet and side of the tub were little reddish dots. Not blood, but wine that had sat in my stomach for too long. I wasn't to the blood stage yet.

I washed my face, shaved, and wet my hair. I put some gel in my hands and looked in the mirror.

"███ you, you piece of ███."

I think there are few things that bring such terror and trepidation to an addict than facing yourself. I looked at myself and the imposter I was and quickly turned away. The hilarity is that I was dressed as if I was planning on changing—dressed as if I cared what happened. I quickly shut off the light and went and sat down on the porch.

I woke back up around noon. The sun high in the sky was evidence of the time of day. Either Coley never came home, or he did and ignored me—conversation between us pointless. He was a good friend with his own life who was dealing with the situation by not coming home a lot and not telling me to get out. I grabbed my box of wine and did a "box stand," pouring the poison directly down my throat from the plug. I stared out at the shed and thought about death, and I smoked.

Only when I stood up did I realize that my pants were soaked. I reached down and grabbed a handful of khaki and inhaled; it wasn't wine. I walked inside and started toward my room when I tripped over the corner of the fireplace and went sprawling into the floor. Tears immediately sprang to my eyes out of anger and fear and worry and rage. I cried for a while sitting on the floor in my urine-soaked pants begging the world to end this misery. When I remembered I was alone, I behaved like a child who thinks no one is looking or listening. I got myself up, brushed off my wounds, and trudged back into my room. Undressing, I stared in my closet, and feeling angry at that moment, I dressed in ridiculously baggy jeans and a black a-frame T-shirt commonly referred to as a "wife beater." I put on a low hat and walked back outside, to the carport this time. I stood on my roommate's son's skateboard and tooled around the pavement, but out of fear of falling as I was unsteady on my feet, I got off and walked back around the house to my wine. I drank, and I drank. I counted my money and realized I was short to buy another box of wine, so I went back inside and stared at the DVDs.

Around ten DVDs were left, and they had to go. Unfortunately, soon I would have to resort to other means to acquire income. I left them and went and drank some more. My box was nearing its bottom, empty and hollow. I was as well, but not empty enough to make a change.

I gathered the movies, filled up my cup, smoked another cigarette, and stared at the door. I was at a level of drunkenness that few people experience. I had been drunk for so many days that normal drunkenness was, well, normal. I was not passed out, so in my mind, it meant that I was at proper operating level. I looked at my phone. I had so many missed calls that I didn't even look at the numbers. I searched the blur of contacts for a specific name—not anyone in particular, just someone I thought wouldn't and didn't judge me. There were not many of those names left. It was around four in the afternoon at this point, and I knew what I had to do. I needed money and more booze and smokes. I needed to see a human being even though I didn't really like them. I got in my car.

This was a little under twenty-four hours in the nightmare that was my life. I have drunk approximately eleven liters of wine; that's the equivalent of five and a half two-liter soda bottles to put it in perspective. I have not eaten in memory. I am an addict. Addicts are a lot like vampires, sucking dry everything in their path, and as I drove down the driveway, I was ready to do anything to fill the emptiness inside.

Chapter 1

1989

The sun was breaking through the blinds just enough for me to know that it was no longer night. I lay under the comforter recognizing the dull buzz of the alarm in my ear, but I did nothing about its insistent tremor. My mother was lying beside me as she had done most nights over the last year. I stretched over her still body and gripped the alarm, silencing its drone. My mind raced over the consequences of my action. Would she care that I made the decision for us to snooze? Would she even realize, when she finally woke, that I had even committed the crime? I nestled back into the covers as the thought drifted from my mind and I went back to sleep.

It seemed like no time at all that the crying alarm in my ear raised me again from slumber. I don't exactly know what snoozes were set to in the eighties, but I am guessing it was just ten minutes or so. I didn't waste any time turning the alarm off, as I knew that there would be consequences for this little boy if I hit the snooze bar again. I reached over her; looking instantly out the window; and then sat up.

I guess it took me about a minute to see that there was an issue. I was preparing to wake her when I noticed something was different about the way that she slept. I spoke her name, as I had done a thousand times.

"Mom"

She didn't move.

"Mom, it's time to get up."

Again, no movement, so I proceeded to shake her.

My mother was a lot of things in life. She was my protector and my constant companion. She was silly, full of curiosity, and extremely funny, especially in the little inside jokes we held between us as only a mother and child can. She loved animals and her children and would go to any length to make sure we were all OK. She was beautiful inside and out, and to me she was all I knew of pure, uncompromised, self-sacrificing, complete love.

What she wasn't was on-time and put together, so for me to have to shake her a few times was normal in the situation.

"Mom, it's time to get up; we are going to be late."

I got no response.

"Mom, wake up!"

It was in the shaking that things changed from normal to abnormal and I recognized the problem, the alarm now appearing in the tightening of my own chest. As I shook her, she started to make an odd noise out of the recesses of her throat. It was a sound that is hard to describe, something between a snore and someone clearing their throat. Whatever it was, it wasn't right. It wasn't anything human or at least anything that I had ever heard in my eleven years on earth or have ever heard since. It was the beginning of a nightmare.

"Mom? . . . Mom . . . Mom . . . MOM!"

The light was coming in the window better by that time, and it seemed my brain recognized the horror all at once. I don't remember if I was sitting or standing on the bed, but all at once I noticed her complexion. Her normal pale freckly skin had turned to a dull shade of blue. Her normally rosy cheeks were the color of Crayola white on a black page. The lips that I knew so well, and had been kissed by a million times, were purple instead of the warm red I had seen since the day I was born.

I shook harder.

"MOM!!!!!!!!"

Her eyelids either opened or I noticed them for the first time, and all I saw was white. I was terrified, but in God's creation of me, He made me a person of action. I leapt from her bed, and in seconds was in my brother's doorway.

My brother, Scott, was a lot like my mother in the sleep department. He would sleep all day if you let him, with his windows blacked out and the fan on, he was just as zombified as her.

"SCOTT, SOMETHING IS WRONG WITH MOM," came blurting out of my mouth in one loud thought.

My brother must have heard something in the inflection of my voice. How many times had I screamed at him to get up just to bother him? I don't know. How many times had I unsuccessfully attempted to mess up his morning with a properly placed yell or tossed something at him to run and hide from his brotherly wrath?

He jumped from bed as if something was pulling him, driving him, like a racehorse frothing after the finish line. He ran past me without a second thought and into her room.

He bolted beside her bed and entered my nightmare with a hair-raising scream. All his adrenalin and fears were confirmed as he saw my mother's condition. His terror was reflected in his now relentless screaming at her, "WAKE UP! MOM, WAKE UP!"

My memory gets a little jumbled at this point. I attempted, over many years, to destroy the plaguing thoughts of these moments with every illegal substance known to man. I remember that Scott approached her and picked up where I left off with the shaking and pleading.

Scott: "Mom, Mom, Mom, Mom! Wake up!"

Scott: "Wake up. What's wrong? MOM, MOM, MOM."

I stood at the end of the bed, closer to the door than I was to her, and watched this with increasing panic. Every bit of normality was gone from the day, and it felt like I was in someone else's life. The picture of her room and bed with her in it are as clear to me as I type this as any photograph burned onto paper.

At some point, Scott looked at me, or I looked at him, and we registered that there was nothing either of us could do in the situation. I don't know who suggested 911, nor do I clearly remember who called.

"911 emergency."

"There is something wrong with my mom; she's not breathing right!"

"Where do you live?"

I gave our address and yelled, "Hurry up. There is something wrong with my mom!"

"You said she is breathing; that's good, I am dispatching an ambulance right now to your residence. They will be there soon; I just need you to stay on the line with me until they get there."

By this time, my brother was hanging halfway out the window screaming for all he was worth, "HHHHEEEELLLLPPPP!!!! HHHHEEEELLLLPPPP!!!!"

I remember he and I trying to do some childlike form of CPR on her. I remember watching her body bounce on the bed. I don't know how long it took the police to respond; it couldn't have been more than a few minutes, but it seemed like an eternity. The seconds dragged on as my brother and I helplessly watched my mother fade out of life.

Eventually, the police drove into the driveway, and I rushed downstairs to get them. With a naïve desire, I thought that if I went outside and pulled, they would get there faster and realize that she was hurt. I guess I didn't think that they would understand the gravity of the situation with a 14-year-old kid hanging halfway out of a second-story window screaming with every ounce of effort in his lungs. I thought that if I got there faster, they would get there faster, and therefore help her faster. I thought they could make this situation go away.

They rushed inside and up the stairs.

Once they assessed the situation, they grabbed her by the shoulders and the feet and tossed her on the floor like the rag doll she was at the time. The image of this scenario plagued my mind for years afterward and became the central image in my trauma memory.

They started performing CPR on her. I can remember standing at the end of the bed looking over the corner at her sprawled out on the carpet. This recollection of standing there watching is and was like an out-of-body experience. I remember it like it was in a movie.

Eventually, the ambulance showed up, and the medics rushed up to help. The last thing that I saw was them ripping her nightgown open to work. I remember the white of her skin and the way her body jostled at each compression. Her nudity was on display for the world.

One officer finally grabbed me and brought me downstairs; I don't know where my brother was at this point. At some point, either the police or one of us called my father who lived nearby, and as I was taken out of the house, he pulled into the driveway. I can distinctly remember standing toward the end of the driveway sobbing into my dad's stomach. My dad, Scott, and I stood there embraced as the ambulance pulled away filled with the uncertainty of whether she would live or die.

My mother wasn't the only thing that left in the ambulance that day. I believe a little of my sanity went with it. Even through a divorce and my father's remarriage, I had kept it together. I took those lumps with the resiliency that children often display through adversities and traumas—all while wounds and bruises are forming quietly under the surface. Yet as my mother's life started to fade out of reality in the back of the ambulance, there was a split in my future. The one filled with butterflies and happiness was killed, extinguished, decimated in a half hour on a May morning in 1989.

I had been rudely awakened to the reality that life is hard and comes at you regardless of what you want or how you think it is going to go or should go. That morning all the shielding that parents do to protect their kids was removed. As my mother was laid bare for the world to see, I saw the world for the first time as it truly was, hard and uncompromising. This was also the moment that I first encountered God in my life. I wouldn't know it for years to come, but as this situation shaped my youth, God was using it to write His story on my soul. In that moment, however, I was just eleven years old. I was lost. I was empty. I was broken. Whatever peace I knew drove away with my mother in the back of an ambulance. As she rode out of sight, so did my innocence and any belief I had in the goodness of the world.

Chapter 2

BROKEN

I find it funny how the strangest things can bring forth such thick and visceral memories, while at other times, the memories that we seek are almost impossible to find. As I sit here writing this sentence, my life is normal from an outside perspective. I am married to a beautiful, kind, and godly woman. My wife and I have two amazing children. I serve in a ministry setting, and my wife works part time serving ladies in our church. The rest of her time, she has selflessly chosen to focus on our children. We spend our weekends playing with the kids, hiking, going on adventures, and working on our home. We are active members in our church and are deeply involved in a small group with people we deeply care about and live life with. We live in the country and are quite happy spending our time outside and in the company of family and friends. We appear normal.

This sense of normalcy was not always the case for me.

After my mother's severe cardiac event, she survived only to have complicated heart problems over several days. Although we spent the first few days at the hospital, I was eventually sent to go stay at my closest friend's house. The Flick family lived in the same neighborhood we did, and Billy had been my best friend from my earliest memory. I felt comfortable being with them and tried to compartmentalize the fact that my mother was lying in a hospital bed close to death, or perhaps I simply didn't understand.

Several days went by. One night I was awakened in the middle of the night and taken to the hospital. I guess the doctors believed that my mother wouldn't survive the night. I remember standing by my mother's bed. She was intubated and couldn't talk, but her eyes were active and confused, and she clearly knew I was there. I recall her trying to talk to me while desperately grasping at the tubes to remove them. I remember crying and not a whole lot else. Eventually, I was whisked out of the room.

My mother survived but not without injury. Due to anoxia, or lack of oxygen to her brain from her repeated heart attacks, she endured what was referred to as brain injury. I have heard multiple explanations for the event, each tainted by the tale-teller's personal angle or motive. I don't know what caused her heart to stop working right. Essentially, the result of the heart attacks was that she had a severely damaged short-term memory, and her long-term memory was on the fritz.

Eventually, she was stabilized and placed in the rehabilitation wing of the hospital to recuperate and for the doctors to determine how much of her ability to function would return. The doctors eventually recognized that this relatively young woman would live the rest of her life as though she had very advanced dementia. My aunt, her sister, would later write a narrative about her experience and entitle it *A Living Hell.*

Sometime after that confusing night, I went to the hospital to see her. I can remember being so overwhelmed with joy that I was going to be with my mom again. We walked into the hospital, and I was met by an imposter. Here was my mother physically. She looked the same. She smelled the same. She had the same dimpled smile and the same laugh. The rest of her was different. At such a young age, I don't think I could have told you what was different, but I could feel it. I remember fearing her, and this dichotomy of emotions worked toward tearing me apart. She had been the person I was most connected to on the planet. She was my greatest advocate, protector, and friend, and yet, the alien in front of me was not her anymore. I was terrified. It was like meeting a stranger that you know is supposed to be your best friend, but you just can't place how you know them or whether you know them. Years later, I watched *Invasion of the Body Snatchers*[1] late one night and noticed that the main character picked up the inconsistencies in his friends in the same way I did with Mom. Something was just off.

Mom could talk, dress herself, do her own hair, and tell stories. But there was something different in her eyes and her soul, and as a child I didn't know how to cope with it. I remember how lost and confused that made me feel.

My brothers were older than me by four and seven years, and although I had known my stepsiblings for a few years, we weren't close at that point in our lives. I am sure someone tried to explain the situation to me, although I do not remember any conversations about Mom's condition. All I thought was that I wanted my mom back to the way she used to be. I think instinctively I knew that was not going to happen.

Trying to adjust to this new reality was not easy for any of us. This blended family went from weekends together to a full-time situation. My stepmother went from a full-time parent of two kids to a full-time parent of five. My mother disappeared into different rehabilitation facilities where they tried to help her to heal from the experience. I saw her rarely in the beginning and even less as the years passed and our distance apart grew. In my childhood confusion, ignoring her reality made coping and adjusting to this new life situation easier. As I aged, I hated myself for that. The moment my mom's brain and body abandoned her, I abandoned her as well.

---

1 *Invasion of the Body Snatchers,* directed by Philip Kaufman (1978; Solofilm; Montreal, Canada).

My dad and stepmom urged us to talk to mom on the phone regularly, write her letters, and visit as appropriate. I rejected these opportunities, as I was allowed to do so. The situation was just too difficult to understand and process, so I avoided it as best as I could. As a kid, I avoided the painful reality through temper tantrums, and as I aged, I avoided it through chemical use. I could not reconcile my two realities: one of safety and love, and one of confusion and lies.

Many years later, my oldest brother and I went to visit her in a facility in Pennsylvania. I think I was sixteen or so, and my brother was in his early twenties. I was old enough to already exist neck-deep in a world of drugs and alcohol. I do not believe I had seen her for about five years at this point.

We pulled into a long drive that wound its way up a small mountain. The winding road up to the facility was surrounded by barren winter trees, desolate and having the appearance of death. The scene was probably exaggerated by my emotional state. As the building came into view, we were staring at a turn-of-the-century sanitorium that had been converted into a hospital for Alzheimer's patients as well as patients with serious brain injuries. It was terrifying.

Walking into the halls of the building was reminiscent of every horror movie I had ever seen. Depressed colors, flickering florescent lights, and old tile floors decorated the halls.

We worked our way down a corridor toward a dayroom and were met by a series of patients; all were characters with bizarre behaviors. Some were sleeping standing up; others were yelling at no one, and others were aimlessly walking and crawling around. When I say it was disturbing, I am not overstating.

Eventually, we went into the dayroom and there sat my mom, smoking a cigarette and happy to see us. I had probably grown a foot since the last time she saw me, probably had a bad haircut, and it is safe to assume I was dressed like a punk. Yet she knew me instantly. Her brain was still on the fritz, but she knew her child.

What an image of God's love for His children. No matter how much we try to mask our identity. No matter how far we run from Him, He knows us.

I don't remember much from the visit other than the horror of the atmosphere and that my brother and I almost got into a fight with a disturbed resident. I think we may have driven my mom to my aunt's house for a visit, but I don't remember for sure.

I do remember leaving. We said our goodbyes and drove about a quarter mile down the winding drive before my brother pulled over. He got out of the car and walked a few steps away to quietly weep. He was so much stronger than I in nearly every regard, but the emotion of the moment took him out. I was already to the point of bottling and masking my feelings. To this day, I struggle to find tears for my own personal issues, but often the waterworks start when I watch a hallmark movie.

After all these years, I still think of my mom going back to that dayroom and sitting there after we were gone. How long was she alone before she forgot we were ever there to begin with? A worse option is to think that she replayed us being there over and over and wondered where we had gone. Did she walk around the facility for hours or days wondering where her children were? Both options make me grieve for her existence during the last season of her life.

Some years ago, I saw a video of a man who had put a Go-Pro on his dog to see what the animal would do when he left for the day. The minute he pulled out of the driveway, the dog began running between windows, watching for his owner to show back up. The video lasted for a long time and at some point, I realized I was crying. I was thinking of Mom. I was imagining her pacing between windows looking for someone she knew. I imagine over the course of her stay in the hospital she probably asked every nurse a thousand times when her family was coming to get her.

Today, I would storm the gates of hell to go and get her and take her home if I could. Back then I was a confused kid, and I didn't show up unless someone made me.

Chapter 3

DIVORCE

I don't remember a lot from my youth and do not have a lot of evidence to bring old memories back to life. Whether I have blocked out those memories or burned them out with drug and alcohol use, I will never know. When I ask others about their experience growing up, they can tell me details about birthday parties and family trips, but I barely remember anything before I was ten years old, and very little after. At holidays, when my family reminisces about events and good memories, it feels as if they are talking about someone else. A few images flash through my head occasionally about an event or a place, but even then, I question whether I am actually remembering something or making something up based on a memory someone else has shared with me. At best these images are two-dimensional, flat and lacking any real clarity or definition. The only memories I recall in great detail are the hard ones.

I had been fine with this reality until I woke up one day and realized that I couldn't remember what my mother sounded like anymore. I couldn't place her voice. Although Mom has been gone for many years, what few memories I have of my early youth revolve almost exclusively around her. The absence of her voice is an absence bigger than any other but God. I have a few pictures of her that give me a momentary flash of a memory, but the memory of her speaking love to me is gone. At times I can feel her voice stirring just beneath the surface of my memory, but it never breaks the surface. My mom's younger sister is still alive and when I talk to Aunt Judy, I get a taste of Mom's voice, but never the real thing. When I am with Aunt Judy, I notice that their smiles and mannerisms are similar as well, but not the same.

One of the oldest solid memories in my brain is the day my parents told me that they were getting divorced. I can't tell you what day it was or why that day was picked. I believe it had to have been a weekend since we were all home together. I am told I was in third grade, but what sticks out to me is the absurdity of the moment. My parents called me out to the screened-in porch on the backside of our house. Now this porch was an important part of our lives, and it does live in my memory. I remember sitting on it with my dad as a summer thunderstorm rolled through one evening. We sat huddled on one of the outdoor vinyl rocking couches while the mist worked its way through the screen and wet our skin. Every time I smell the rain, I am reminded of that evening, and it drives me to have similar experiences with my children. Dad and I would count the seconds between light and noise to figure out the distance of the approaching lightning. I also remember eating during cookouts on that porch as my dad grilled his famous London broil, charred on the outside and perfectly cooked on its interior. In my spotty memory, this porch was a centerpiece of the life of our family.

On the day in question, I followed my parents out to the porch and found both my brothers sitting there crying. My parents proceeded to tell me that they were getting divorced, but as a little kid I don't remember understanding the gravity of what they were saying. I knew it was serious and was desperately trying to stifle my laughs. I wasn't laughing because of the divorce; I was laughing because both of my super strong untouchable older brothers were sobbing. They were and still are two of the strongest men I know, and here were these two giants in my life bawling.

Eventually, the impact of the moment sank in as my dad moved out and into a condo across town. Other than his exit from the house, nothing seemed to change for a little while. I played with my toys. I played with our dog. I tried to play with my older brothers. I rode my bike and did all the things I had done previously. The world had shifted on its axis, but it was mostly lost on me.

With the destruction of the nuclear family in America and the artificial advancement of the maturity levels of our youth today, I think a third grader today would have a better grasp on the situation than I had; for me divorce was a mostly foreign concept. The difference is that I was truly innocent at the time. My life revolved around very little other than play, fun, and love, and I was shielded from the world to the best of my mother's ability. It wasn't until decades later that I learned that my parents had been fighting a lot in the months and years leading up to their divorce. My brothers were not as shielded as I was, and they carry the scars from those memories.

When I was a preteen, I remember going to a friend's house to spend the night, and I saw his parents kissing in their kitchen. These adults were embraced in affection and were expressing that through playful kisses and hugs. In that moment, standing in my friend's house, I realized that I had never seen my parents kiss. It wasn't odd to me that they weren't affectionate because I didn't know anything different. Seeing a more physical affection between two married adults was a stark contrast to the family experience that played in the movie reel in my head, and honestly in the moment, I felt a little embarrassed as if I was seeing something that was wrong. My parents hadn't held hands, hugged, kissed, or at least they never did in front of me that I can remember.

As I have thought about this, I realize that I have seen much more affection in my dad's marriage to my stepmother. They often hugged and kissed. They enjoy each other in a way that was not displayed for me to see in my parents' marriage. The reasons for my parents' lack of affection do not matter. I do however see that God has called me to something different with my own family.

Today, as my wife and I are prepping dinner in the kitchen with our two beautiful children sitting at the table, we are often playful, attacking each other, or giving hugs and kisses. My daughter will start crying if I tickle Mommy, as she wants to protect her mom. I am not saying that all married couples should smooch in front of their kids, but I am suggesting that my children will always know that I love their mother, in both words and action. I know God has called me to pursue my wife as God has also called me to give my son and daughter an example of what that looks like. I don't know all the factors that led to my parents' divorce, and I really don't care at this point. At the end of the day, it doesn't matter to me in that God is using the truths I have found in their situation to create change in mine.

Regardless of the reasons, I think it is fair to assume that one or both of them stopped pursuing the other. I also know that this is easy to do as life gets busy with kids, activities, and exhaustion. The economy God places us in is one where there is one truth to the order of priorities He wants for us: God, then spouse, then kids, then everything else.

I need to pursue God with all my heart, love my wife as Christ loved the church, and raise my kids to understand that eternal reality. If I don't, and they come to know the Lord, they will eventually figure out that I dropped the ball. If I earnestly pursue God and Lauren, then my risk of losing everything else significantly drops, but this takes a substantial amount of intentionality. I have to love hard enough that my kids know what that means and then they hopefully will not try to find love in all the wrong places as I did.

This is not just something God has called me to do; this is something I get to do. Often in life, especially in ministry, we feel the pressure to serve others and end up neglecting our own family, those who love us the most. This unintentional consequence of busyness happens every day to people in all walks of life. One spouse gets caught up in something that seems important, and neglects something that is not only very important, but might have generational impacts.

Several years ago, while I was in the process of being considered as Miracle Hill's next CEO, Lauren and I had dinner with Reid and Barbara Lehman. Toward the end of that dinner, Barbara shared some wisdom with my wife, cautioning us, cautioning me specifically. She said, "You two need to be careful to not sacrifice your life and your family on the altar of ministry." If we are not careful, we can justify everything we do as necessary. In a ministry setting, this is even more pronounced as we are engaged in doing something for others that has an eternal impact and seems more than worthy of our time. Frankly, this is an excuse that is used for us to validate doing what we want to do.

We don't want to wind up being the person justifying to Jesus all the great stuff that we did and then have Him confirm in that moment that it wasn't for Him.

> Not everyone who says to me, "Lord, Lord," will enter the kingdom of heaven, but the one who does the will of my Father who is in heaven. On that day many will say to me, "Lord, Lord, did we not prophesy in your name, and cast out demons in your name, and do many mighty works in your name?" And then will I declare to them, "I never knew you; depart from me, you workers of lawlessness."
>
> —Matthew 7:21–23

As a child I didn't realize that the domino of divorce was the first of a few dominoes over the next few years that would work to alter my course in life. I don't know what would have been different if that domino had not fallen, but I am committed to change the paradigm for my own children. I have heard both of my brothers, and many children of divorce, say basically the same thing over the years. None of us know the intimate details in someone else's marriage or frankly know exactly what is going on in the mind of our spouse, but we do know and have control over our own thoughts and actions. We are only responsible for what we can do to make our marriages healthy, and that starts with putting our greatest resources—time and energy—into the relationships that we know and value as most important.

Chapter 4

FIRST DRINK

There are a lot of differing opinions about the root cause of addiction. If you look at it historically, one of the oldest theories is the moral model which states that there is something inherently wrong with an individual's character—that they are weak-willed and the problem cannot be corrected. The moral model can be summarized by the idea that once you are a pickle, you can never be a cucumber again. This was the prevailing model for over a millennium, until the beginning of the twentieth century and the creation of the disease model. The disease model says that a person with an addiction has a disease that cannot be cured, only treated. This is the root belief of the AA movement led by Dr. Bob S. and Bill W.

In the latter half of the twentieth century, a myriad of models took shape as a result of the scientific boom. There is the learned behavior model, which points to the environment a person grows up or evolves within. There is a genetic predisposition model, which shows addiction as a preset marker in the genetic soup that makes you, you. The family of origin model encourages us to look to our family tree to identify the root of our issues. The addictive personality model says that we are hardwired toward passion and when passion takes root, it can develop into obsession, fixation, and eventually addiction. At Miracle Hill if you ask us which model is correct, we will say, yes.

Certainly, the easy thing to point to is sin and idolatry. There is no doubt that at its root, addiction is idolatry. The harder conversation has to do with why a person goes to this empty well specifically.

Humans are not so simple that we can point to a singular reason for their addictions and life-dominating issues. Rather, helpers are called to meet people at their point of brokenness and be Jesus to them in their pain and trauma. Through an intentionally built relationship, we then help them to examine their own lives to determine the contributing issues they need to address. All the while we should be pointing them toward the loving arms of Jesus, the true salve and medicine we believe they need.

In my own life I have sought to learn who I am and what makes me tick. In my recovery journey I was encouraged to examine my history and experiences to find the root causes of my behaviors. This inventorying of life is something I do to this day, and as a Christian, I believe this is a necessary step toward sanctification. All who know Jesus should be yearning to be like Him, and as a result, we should not walk around with blinders on, but we should daily examine why we do what we do.

When I reflect on my addiction, I can see a relationship with mind-altering chemicals that was out of whack from the first instance I had an opportunity to use. I can't remember exactly what year it was, but I believe it was the summer between sixth and seventh grade when I got drunk for the first time. My grandfather had recently been moved to the Upstate as he was aging and needed more specific care for his Alzheimer's disease. During the transition, his belongings, that he couldn't take into the new home, were placed in a big pile in our garage. I remember snooping through the remains of his worldly belongings and finding a very expensive leather double flask. I recognized that it contained alcohol but did not know what type of alcohol it was initially.

I clearly knew that I wasn't supposed to have it. I stole it anyway. Years later, as my palate for booze developed, I had a sip of bourbon that instantly whisked me back to that moment. Bourbon is like liquid fire and the resulting story was like gasoline on an ember.

Once I was in possession of my grandfather's flasks of brown liquor, I had to determine what to do with it. I did what any degenerate newly traumatized youth does in that situation, I looked for a few buddies to include in my plan.

That night, two of my friends and I went into the woods behind my house to camp. I think this may have been the first time I was allowed to camp outside without a parent. After some coaxing, my friends and I drank a flask of bourbon and as you can imagine, we quickly became quite drunk. We stumbled around the camp. We threw up on each other, and we generally had a terrible time.

The next morning my friends rode home on their bikes, christened with newly earned merit badges as well as raging hangovers. I went inside, called up another set of friends, and that night we drank the rest of the bourbon.

This would be my general modus operandi for the remainder of my career as a user. I would use as many drugs and as much alcohol as was available until it was gone. I would burn through one set of friends until they tucked their tails between their legs and went home. I would use alcohol, drugs, people, places, and things until they were in a rubble of ash.

Early in recovery, I was challenged by the idea that I would have to find people who don't use any drugs or alcohol at all. Knowing the prevalence and acceptance of alcohol in society, I didn't think there was anyone who lived a completely sober existence. Even considering the church, my perception was that most people drink and do so often. While I now know that there are a lot of people who live life sober, I also know that there is a larger group of people who drink socially but are not owned by the substance. It was in this recognition that I realized that my relationship to alcohol was different from that of others.

Both of my brothers are social drinkers. My brother Scott will buy a six-pack of some type of IPA, and it will sit in his fridge for a month. He will drink one beer, and the rest will just sit there. Two months later, he might drink two more. A few months after that, he will open a beer, not drink it and pour it down the sink. This type of equation doesn't compute for me. When I used a substance, I used it all, whatever it was and whatever was available, until it was gone. The idea of sipping a beer is a concept that is as foreign to me as speaking Yiddish.

In my brain I couldn't fathom the point of alcohol if it wasn't to get drunk. When I went to a bar with a friend and that person set down a half empty beer or mixed drink as we headed to another pub, I would come behind them and down their drink until there wasn't a drop left. I thought that leaving a drink behind was a crime or that the person was trying to stay sober. This was my thought process and in the midst of my madness, this made sense to me. In fact, that person most likely had a healthy relationship with intoxicating substances.

I just wasn't built that way. Perhaps some of the trauma of my youth rewired my brain in this capacity. Perhaps it was my deep need for acceptance. Perhaps it was a personality issue. Regardless, my relationship to intoxicants and narcotics is different than most.

I think this is true for most of the men and women who come through Miracle Hill and who struggle with addiction issues. This is not to eliminate their personal choice in the matter, but it is worth noting the difference in how individuals relate to substances. When comparing my drinking to some of you reading this, we are not talking about the same thing. Yes, it is the same action with the same substance, but I didn't come with a governor on the engine.

In the early years of recovery, I struggled greatly to cope with the alcohol and drug use I saw in the world around me. The craving to feel a certain way, or not at all, can be overwhelming to someone in early recovery. With relapse rates as high as they are, we have to examine what would cause so many people to choose to go back to this type of existence. There are a million reasons, but often they believe that they can shift their relationship to alcohol and handle it the same way most of society does. They desperately want to be or be perceived as normal, whatever that means. Furthermore, alcohol provides them with something that they cannot seem to find in the world, momentary peace.

Some people would even say, "As you become more and more like Jesus, there is a chance that He will deliver you from your addiction and redeem your relationship to substances." In this scenario the logical conclusion would be that you can return to social use. This dichotomy becomes an argument in Christian recovery circles, and some might chastise you for saying, "Hello, I'm Ryan, and I am an addict." The question is: Am I an addict or am I delivered? The challenge from some might be that I am unaccepting of God's faithfulness to deliver me from my sin. If I do not spout the word *deliverance*, then do I believe His word?

I do. For me, there is risk if I take my eyes off the reality of what my relationship to substances has been in the past. The only way for me to find out if my deliverance is true is to have a drink. I have no interest in that experiment. I will live a sober life and frankly, at this point, I don't want anything else. I see the destruction that alcohol and drugs do to people and families every day of my life. Not just in our shelters, but in the world, and specifically in the Church. I will consider myself delivered the day I die sober and am face to face with Jesus.

If you are someone with a healthy relationship to alcohol, God bless you. It seems to me that the Bible speaks against drunkenness but not against drinking. However, if you know Jesus and you know addicts, be aware. Someone else's relationship to alcohol might not be the same as yours, and you could accidentally be a stumbling block to those around you. I know you would never intentionally do that, but by expressing your "freedom in Christ," you might be contributing to a deep wound in someone else's life. Additionally, make no mistake, your freedom in Christ can be something that becomes an idol. If that is true, then it's not freedom at all. It's just something in your own life in which you are finding counterfeit peace.

When I find myself in a meeting with those in recovery and I have an opportunity to share with the group, I typically say, "Hi, my name is Ryan, and I am a grateful believer in Jesus Christ, saved by His grace, and I am in recovery from my addiction, sin, and guilt." The most important part of identifying ourselves is through our identity in Christ; everything else is details and semantics.

For those who are still struggling in their addictions, there is a different way, a higher power, a path to peace, and His name is Jesus. Stick around, and we will learn more about Him as the chapters progress.

Chapter 5

DIVE

My path in addiction started and ended at the bottom of a bottle. Along the way, social use evolved into addiction, and every moral barrier was crossed. Once the first bottle of bourbon was empty, it wasn't a year before I smoked weed for the first time. By the end of my journey, there was not a drug that I had not used, nor a moral line that I had not crossed.

When I was in middle school, weed was still very much considered a drug. Unlike today, weed was looked down upon by most people, including students, and was a long way from the politically and socially accepted intoxicant it is today.

During the seventh grade, one of my friends invited me to spend the night at his house one weekend. He told me that he had a surprise for me. I eventually pulled it out of him that we were going to smoke a joint. The rest of that week was filled with excitement while I wrestled with the idea of crossing this invisible boundary. I didn't know what pot would do, but I knew it was off limits. I had been told my whole life during Red Ribbon Week that doing drugs was both illegal and wrong. My excitement won the internal argument, and I decided to see what all the fuss was about.

As a twelve-year-old kid, I had already crossed a bunch of boundaries. I was smoking cigarettes as quickly as I could steal them and drinking frequently when the opportunity arose. All this was wrong, and I knew it. Every source of wisdom in my life told me to not use drugs. While I recognized in my head that heroin and crack were in a different category of wrong, all these experiences were clearly labeled as off limits.

The weekend came, and we got high. Nothing crazy happened through the experience. We played video games at the mall, and I struggled to understand what was on the screen with my visual and auditory experience heightened from the THC. We played volleyball at someone's house. I threw up in another guy's truck in a McDonald's Drive Thru.

Once home the next day, I called a bunch of my neighborhood friends who were eager to hear of the experience. I met them at one of our hangout spots in the woods. I proceeded to tell them the story, and they looked at me in amazement. I had done drugs, and I perceived that I was cooler and better as a result. Nothing bad had happened to me and in fact, I felt like I had matured due to the experience. The emotional high I got from my friends' reactions was as good as smoking the weed, maybe better. Weed became a regular part of my life after that weekend.

I think it is fair to note that most of my family life was as healthy as it could be. My dad, Steve, and stepmother, Nancy, had their hands full with five kids after my mother's illness. They provided a great life for all of us, and I never wanted for anything. As an adult, I have thought more about how difficult it must have been for the two of them to rearrange life for five kids. Nancy was in a hard spot with the addition of three wounded boys, and she did an amazing job caring for all of us in a hard situation. I remember how much she tried to get me to call my mom. She bought my mom birthday gifts over the years and mailed them to her from us. She not only tried to make life OK, but she tried to make sure we honored our mother as we coped with our own issues.

My stepsiblings, Mary and Eric, whom I had known at a distance for years before our parents got married, went from having a house to themselves most days, to complete chaos in the blink of an eye. We all ate dinner together most nights. We had extravagant vacations and bountiful piles of presents at Christmas. Compared to so many kids who grow up surrounded by tragedy and poverty, I had it good. But that didn't change what was going on in my heart and mind.

Once I entered high school, drugs went from a random occurrence to a regular part of the week. I drank every weekend and smoked weed most weekends. In high school, I smoked weed every day before school, on breaks, and after school. Marijuana use colored the world I saw around me and was a focus of my actions each day. As a kid I thought that I was hiding the use from my teachers and coaches. As an adult I know there is no way that this was true. They would have to have been blind to not see the shift in my glazed eyes and performance in the classroom. I recall that my friends and I sometimes met in the school parking lot and smoked a joint or two before going to our high school physics class. We would keep the windows up and the air conditioning set on recirculation to heighten the effect, and subsequently paint the whites of our eyes the color of a stop sign. There is no way I didn't smell like a giant joint when I rolled into class and watched dumbfounded as the physics teacher performed what appeared to be gravity defying experiments.

The wrongness of each drug wore off the moment that nothing bad happened after using it. One day someone had a bag of cocaine. I used it and nothing bad happened. One day I was offered a pill. I took it. Nothing bad happened. Over the course of four years, I took **all** the pills, every kind I could try. By the end of high school, I had a regular supply of Ritalin to snort each day. This helped to combat the depressed mood from being stoned. Economically, drug users at this stage are communal in their efforts. If I had a bag of weed, then so did everyone else. Some kids got ADHD medication, which meant I had access as well. I would take one drug to get stoned and then crush and snort another to even out. I was a mess, but it seemed completely normal to me, and no one told me differently.

There were certainly eyes of judgment from the more balanced kids, but social pressures have a way of both keeping someone stuck as well as keeping people from speaking the truth. My need for acceptance might have overruled my desire to get high had my out-of-control behavior been confronted by my peer group, but it wasn't. At least not while I was sober and could remember it.

One weekend I gave a friend ten dollars to get us a dime bag of weed for the weekend. When he picked me up, he handed me two tabs of LSD, white blotter. Acid doesn't look like much of anything. The blotter tabs of acid in those days were the size of an eraser tip on the end of a pencil. I took the acid, had a wild ride for twelve hours, and went home. Nothing bad had happened other than another hard drug used, and a barrier crossed.

By the end of high school, I thought nothing bad had happened to me. In reality I had dropped out of all sports. I failed two courses my senior year, which prevented me from graduating. I had been ticketed several times for possession of alcohol by a minor and possession of marijuana. I had totaled two cars. My dad and stepmother were at the end of their ropes, and I was days from being asked to leave my home.

Nothing bad had happened to me other than all that.

Is there such a thing as a gateway drug? Yes. It is simpler than that though. Sin begets sin. The easier it is for us to partake in one sin, the easier it is to do something different, more dangerous, and more compromising to our innocence.

Although I failed out of school, I did attend my class graduation. I showed up drunk and high and watched my friends walk across the stage. I don't know why I subjected myself to this torture. I walked into the auditorium and had to interact with all my friends' parents. They asked me what I was doing, and I had to explain my shame. The drugs numbed the experience, but as I lay down to sleep that night, I could remember only their eyes of pity and judgment. Perhaps some of what I perceived from them wasn't true, but much of it was real and deserved.

Shortly thereafter, things came to a head at home and my dad forced me to leave. A typically tense interaction with my father had exploded due to my decisions and disrespect. I ran out of the house that I had called a home and for the next year, I moved from one couch to the next. I wouldn't lay my head on a pillow in my family home for nearly fifteen years. It was during this season that I experienced true homelessness for the first time.

After my removal from my parents' house, I couch surfed at different families' homes, and I wore out my welcome at several. Remember these were all recent high school graduates, so their homes were their parents' homes. A friend named Josh stayed with me one evening as I made calls and tried to find somewhere else to go. I could not go to his house, and no one else was answering their phones. I was out of options. That evening he took me to a nearby business park that had some large fields and open areas. He told me he would be back for me in the morning and left me standing there. I had no jacket or sleeping bag and was truly going to have to sleep rough.

I walked around the park and saw that there was a brick maintenance shed toward the back. Once I reached the shed, I realized that I couldn't get in. There were some large holly bushes around the shed and upon further inspection, I saw that the bushes grew in such a way that they created large open cavities in their interior. I settled in the best that I could under the biggest of these bushes. The time seemed to slow, but eventually I went to sleep.

In the middle of the night, I was awakened to a sound.

Brrrrrr-it-it-it-it-it-it-it
Brrrrrr-it-it-it-it-it-it-it
Brrrrrr-it-it-it-it-it-it-it

I could not place the sound at first until the water made its way through the prickly leaves and started to fall on my head and shoulders. The sprinklers had come on and were adding insult to my existing injury. The wetness in addition to the cooling nature of night created a miserable bed—one I both deserved and hated at the same time. I crawled further back into the bushes, the pointed leaves sticking into my skin, but I found a dry spot and eventually went back to sleep as the water from the sprinklers mixed with my tears. For the remaining hours of the night, I slept little, begging the night to be over and the sun to rise.

Once awake and mobile again, I walked to the front of the park and waited for Josh to show back up. During this time and many times after I played out my situation in my head.

What if he doesn't come back?
Where am I going to go?
Will he have anything to eat?
What am I going to do?

He showed up that day, but there were many days when no one did. I was the author of my situation, and it continually went downhill. This is what can happen when you are the god of your own life.

In the fall of that year, I found myself living on a couch in a dorm apartment at the University of South Carolina Upstate Campus. Several of my friends were going to school there and living in a shared housing apartment, and they let me stay there for several months. I did not do anything during that time to better myself. I used and drank and partied. I was like a leech that would suck the blood out of anyone who was kind enough to let me. One day, several months into my stay there, I went over to another guy's apartment to smoke a blunt and play Tecmo Bowl on Nintendo. We were sitting there stoned out of our minds when the front door to the room was kicked in, and the police entered. What I did not know is that one of the roommates was stealing backpacks and selling textbooks. The police had come to serve a search warrant. Within seconds I was handcuffed and thrown in the back seat of the police car. In transit to the jail, the other guy in the back seat was franticly trying to take drugs out of his shirt pockets to shove into the cracks and crevices of the backseat of the police car. This is not something that is done solo when you are in handcuffs, so I helped.

I was arrested on a slew of charges, given a trespass notice for the campus for life, and sent to big boy jail. As the door to the holding cell slammed shut, I recognized that I probably wasn't getting out of this scenario easily.

For the first time in my life, I was headed to a county jail without the hope of receiving a ticket and being sent on my way. Soon I was processed and moved to my home for the next few months at the Spartanburg County Jail-Annex. As I went to sleep in my bunk that first night, all that was on my mind was how I could salvage what I created. I couldn't come up with a reasonable answer.

A few weeks later, with desperation and Thanksgiving approaching, I found the courage to call my family. The phone was answered by my oldest brother who had little to no pity for me, and he quickly handed the phone to my father. Making myself as small as possible in the cell, I begged and pleaded, sobbing quietly for someone to pay my bail and to come and get me. He did what he should have done in that situation and said no. I was released a few months later, a little bit more street-smart and a lot less willing to change. All I could think of doing was getting high to numb the pain and find a little bit of peace. No longer was I scared of jail or getting arrested. I believed in my heart that my family didn't want me; no one did as far as I could tell, so I committed to doing whatever I wanted in life.

This led me down a dark and dangerous path infused with crime, sex, drugs, and debauchery.

The heart is deceitful above all things, and desperately sick; who can understand it?

—Jeremiah 17:9

Some years later, I found myself living in the true underbelly of society. By the time the nineties were flipping over to the double aughts, I was using daily and living for the weekends when I would use harder and harder drugs at the rave clubs that had sprouted up over the previous decade. I would get off work on Friday if I had a job and immediately get whatever drugs were popular and readily available at the time. Use would start immediately, and I would stop using when the drugs ran out, typically days later.

Like chemists, we would mix different drugs to heighten their effect. Candy flipping, which is combining ecstasy and LSD, typically started early on Fridays and was sometimes a regular occurrence throughout the week. On this cocktail, the whole world would morph out of reality for half a day or longer. The ability to discern what was real and what was a figment of my hallucinating overcooked imagination would fizzle out for an extended period of time. The most basic human interactions became a challenge. To reduce the risk of losing the high, we would simply double down on the concoctions to make them last for consecutive days. Each added compound worsened the risk for overdose and death, but I did not care or even think about life in terms of life or death. The question was simply how to keep the high going. We would hide from the sun, scared of the truth it would tell us. Some weeks the psychoactive drugs would taint my mind in such a way that I could not tell when and if I got sober. While my body thinned out due to lack of nutrition, my skin bleached from the absence of vitamin D. Those around me and I became the walking dead.

What I saw around me was a cacophony of strobe lights and glow sticks—all light sources giving a glowing delayed tracer effect, like fireflies in a dark sky. The thrum of the bass from the music became the heartbeat of my bruised and battered soul. The bass was more a feeling than a sound and for days after, my body would vibrate as waves do the day after you leave the beach. The ability to discern what I was seeing and how far my life had degraded would be lost in the light and noise.

I would walk into a home, warehouse, or club late on a Friday night and reemerge some days later not knowing what time or day it was. My body would be coated with a layer of salt and mixed sweat from the dancing and churning of human on human, our body fluids mixed together much like the drugs. When we exited, it didn't mean the party stopped; it just meant it moved somewhere more intimate—somewhere away from prying eyes and where indecency has no limitations.

Sleep was a hindrance to the party, so we didn't do it. Into the mix went opiates and cocaine and ketamine, methamphetamine, mushrooms, and crack. Alcohol and marijuana were always present and looking back, whole years went into the abyss of drug-fueled frenzy.

- What would I do to get the drugs? Anything.
- Who would I hurt to accomplish my goals? Anyone.
- What line was too far to cross? For a long time, it was the needle, but eventually I was shown that peace could be achieved faster and easier when injected.

Human interaction became transactional and in the absence of love, physical intimacy became a counterfeit currency traded like used baseball cards. Sexuality became undefined, and human eroticism knew no bounds. All of this to what end? There was no purpose or value other than self-gratification and escape.

The things I did to maintain this lifestyle are abhorrent, and I won't elevate the evil of my life by writing the details on these pages. When I say I am now a sinner saved by grace, oh what a sinner I have been, and how big God's grace is. The Bible teaches us the three most important things we can do: love God, love others, and tell everyone about Jesus.

And he said to him, "You shall love the Lord your God with all your heart and with all your soul and with all your mind. This is the great and first commandment. And a second is

like it: You shall love your neighbor as yourself. On these two commandments depend all the Law and the Prophets.
—Matthew 22:37–40

And Jesus came and said to them, "All authority in heaven and on earth has been given to me. Go therefore and make disciples of all nations, baptizing them in the name of the Father and of the Son and of the Holy Spirit, teaching them to observe all that I have commanded you. And behold, I am with you always, to the end of the age.
—Matthew 28:18–20

The opposite of these precious truths is found in the idea that we should do whatever fancies us in the moment. Aleister Crowley, occultist and founder of the religion of Thelema, said in 1904, "Do what thou wilt shall be the whole of the law." [1]What he meant was that it is each person's responsibility to do whatever is right in their own mind, whenever they want to do it according to their own determined path.

This view points to the idea that man's highest achievement is to follow one's own will regardless of what others think, what is morally acceptable, or who it hurts. This position is self-obsessed and based on the idea that "I know best." In essence, we then become our own god. Whether conscious or unconscious, addiction leads people into this frame of understanding about their life. While the obvious object of idolization is the drug, the reality is that the true idol becomes self.

---

1 Aleister Crowley, *The Book of the Law* (Anubis Books, 2018), chap. 1, iBooks.

Chapter 6

WHO ARE YOU?

The American Psychological Association (APA) defines *personal identity* as, "an individual's sense of self defined by (a) a set of physical, psychological, and interpersonal characteristics that is not wholly shared with any other person and (b) a range of affiliations (e.g., ethnicity) and social roles." [1] The APA says that identity formation happens as we age and is most prominent in emerging adulthood, ages eighteen to twenty-five. As one's identity is being formed, the brain is developing simultaneously. The prefrontal cortex, the area responsible for decision-making, right behind your forehead, finishes its development also at age twenty-five. This means that kids and young adults under twenty-five do not have a good grasp on who they are or how to get where they want to go. They are grasping at anchors in their world to keep them in place, and to tell them something about themselves. I was no different.

As an additional step toward weakening my grasp on personal identity, I added in copious amounts of alcohol and drugs to cook my

---

1 *APA Dictionary of Psychology* (2024), s.v. "identity." https://dictionary.apa.org/identity.

brain and stunt my emotional development. What was left was a zombie, with the maturity of a toddler, walking around in a full-grown body.

As young children, we either understand our identity as a reflection of those closest to us or as a mixture of physical characteristics, or both. This very rudimentary understanding of self is colored by the environment we find ourselves in and the people who surround us and love us.

It is easy for me to see that I had no clue who I was when I began to experiment with drugs and alcohol. Just a few years earlier, even though younger, I believe I would have had a much easier time defining myself in the world around me. I was a part of a family. I was an athlete like my brothers. I had two parents who loved me. I had a dog, Sailor, who told me daily through the wag of his tail that I was amazing. I was a normal kid with curly hair, curious about the world around me.

As my perception of stability shifted, I struggled to understand my place in a world that I thought was covered in shifting sand. Ever increasing levels of toxins and solvents coursing through my blood with increasing regularity complicated an already complicating puzzle.

Throughout my teens and into my twenties, I would define myself almost solely based on appearance and as a reflection of whatever friend group I had at the time, much like a toddler does in child development.

As I moved from elementary to middle school, I viewed popularity and "being liked" as the main purpose in education. School came easy to me, which allowed me to put my focus on the social dynamics of education. Perhaps I thought that if others thought well of me, then that meant that I was well. I evaluated my own worth as the sum of what I thought others viewed me as. Most kids about to enter their early preteens have similar thoughts. Kids whose lives are grounded elsewhere in familial and relational stability have a much easier time distinguishing the real from the counterfeit. I could not make that distinction and worked very hard to ensure people thought I was cool. I tried so hard to find identity in the approval of others that I "overtried" and often wore out my welcome. As I moved through middle school, I perceived that I did not fit in anywhere I went.

It turns out that misery loves company, and I eventually found a tribe on the island of misfit toys. As the years went by in middle school and into high school, I found myself surrounded by other kids who also struggled with their identity and were willing to experiment with the boundaries of the world to find it. In our isolation from the socially acceptable, we found acceptance in each other. In our countercultural behaviors, we found what we thought was freedom from the world.

Let this serve as a warning to parents. If you do not provide stability to your children, they will look for it elsewhere. If you are not present in their lives, they will find someone who is. If you develop no depth in relationship with them such that they know they can trust you, they will search the heavens to find a reflection of their worth, and they will not care about your artificially set boundaries.

We knew less about ourselves as the years went on, but the marijuana- and alcohol-infused haze made it matter much less. Each day, we lost boys and girls acted as hunter-gatherers, scrounging up change to have some older person buy us booze. We conjured imaginative ways to steal cigarettes and adult magazines from the local pharmacy, and then we retreated to the woods to live in our own world. We could not see the danger around us, and no one was there to tell us.

As the years progressed, so did the drugs and my state of personal confusion. As the boundaries of acceptable behavior were eliminated and the distance from my family grew, my ideals for appearance and hygiene shifted.

When I was fifteen or so, a friend of mine tattooed a small cross on my arm with Indian ink and a needle. Over the following few days, I lived in a state of constant panic thinking that my dad would see it, imagining the disappointment he would express. I knew my family expected something different from me as all my siblings had charted the acceptable course ahead of me. Essentially, the map said I was supposed to stay relatively morally clean and get through high school before moving on to college. I knew this was the expectation for my future self.

A few days later, I had a friend use a toothbrush, salt, and lemon juice to try to scrape the tattoo out of me. After an hour of pain, I wound up with a permanent scar, a gaping wound, and a faded tattoo once it healed.

Around the age of seventeen, I had a keg party one night when my parents were out of town. I invited essentially the whole school, and we had a "rager" at the house. Some girl's older brother showed up during the party with what I perceived as a legit tattoo kit. After looking through his book of flash art I picked out the head of a wolf and had him tattoo it right over the scar on my arm. He was trying to learn to tattoo so he traded the tattoo for access to the tap of the keg. For the record, the last thing you want your tattoo artist to be is drunk. I was too young to understand this principle.

Whereas I had previously been scared of having a tiny tattoo and the wrath of disappointment I would receive, I no longer cared what anyone thought. What a difference a few years had made as I chose to put this giant permanent decision into my skin. The artist suggested that we elongate the fangs and add some extra whiskers to make the wolf look meaner. I agreed, thinking this was a great idea.

The next morning, I woke up with a horrible hangover, not remembering much from the night before. I walked around the house picking up the array of beer cans and trash and thought someone must have punched me in the arm or perhaps I had fallen the night before. I didn't remember the tattoo at all.

Once the trash was cleaned up, I went to the bathroom to take a shower. I undressed and did a double take in the mirror. Staring back at me was what appeared to be the head of a sewer rat. My friends began regularly laughing about Ryan's Master Splinter tattoo. The leader of the Teenage Mutant Ninja Turtles now had a permanent place on my arm. Even today if I run into someone I haven't seen in thirty years, they will laughingly ask, "Do you still have Master Splinter on your arm?" I didn't try to hide it from anyone including my family. I was learning that the crazier I looked, the easier it was to keep people away. The more my identity was dependent on others, the more I felt rejected by others. The more I felt rejected, the more I retreated into the perceived safety of being different. If people perceived me as not caring, then maybe I truly wouldn't care. At least they wouldn't see how much I did care.

A year later I put gauged earrings in both ears and my tongue. Two years later both nipples. My body became a road map of bad tattoos, scars, and poor decision-making. I thought that with every external adjustment, I would know who I was better. I didn't.

With every choice I believed I was creating some unique individual that would tell people what I was about without me ever having to say a word. With each choice separating me from "normal," I was choosing to define myself by what those around me chose as their definition. In fact, we were all doing the same thing, thinking we were being different. We wanted to be perceived as living outside the box, when we were truly putting ourselves into smaller and smaller boxes.

By my early twenties, the fog of addiction mixed with my underdeveloped self had left me open to increasingly dangerous decision-making and isolation from society. I wasn't even a shadow of the man I thought I wanted to be as I lay in my bed as a child dreaming of flying fighter jets in the Air Force or fixing hearts in a surgical suite. The American dream of family and stability was replaced with an American nightmare where I was lost in a pitch-black labyrinth asking, "*Who am I?*" again.

In Chapter 5 of Lewis Carroll's famed fantasy, *Alice's Adventures in Wonderland,* Alice finds herself in an identity crisis. As she struggles to understand what is happening to her, she comes upon a hookah-smoking caterpillar:

> The Caterpillar and Alice looked at each other
> for some time in silence: at last, the Caterpillar took the

hookah out of its mouth, and addressed her in a languid, sleepy voice.

"Who are **you**?" said the Caterpillar.

This was not an encouraging opening for a conversation. Alice replied, rather shyly, "I—I hardly know, sir, just at present —at least I know who I WAS when I got up this morning, but I think I must have been changed several times since then."

"What do you mean by that?" said the Caterpillar sternly. "Explain yourself!"

"I can't explain **myself**, I'm afraid, sir," said Alice, "because I'm not myself, you see."[2]

I sure have felt like Alice in the past, unable to define myself, know how I got where I was, and at the same time understanding that I was not myself at all.

Famed psychologist Erik Erikson said, "A well-developed identity is comprised of goals, values, and beliefs to which a person is committed. It is the awareness of the consistency in self over time, as well as the recognition of this consistency by others." [3] I had no values, unless the absence of values is a value itself. I had no goals other than to survive to get high the next day. My only belief in the world was that it was harsh and unforgiving. To top it off, I was committed to nothing and no one, a vagabond chameleon vampire, transforming into anything necessary to suck the life out of those around me. By keeping people at arm's length or by pushing them away, I didn't have anyone who would challenge me to change.

Over the years, several people tried to help, no one more so than my brothers, although they often didn't know what to do. They each let

---

2 Lewis Carroll, *Alice's Adventures in Wonderland* (New York: T. Y. Crowell & co, 1893), 48.
3 Erik Erikson, "Identity Development Theory," Lumen, accessed July 12, 2023, https://courses.lumenlearning.com/adolescent/chapter/identity-development-theory/.

me live with them; Chris and my sister-in-law Kelly let me into their home twice. Each time, Chris sat me down and helped me come up with a plan for success. I would morph into his expectation for a season, but by then addiction had its roots in my decisions. The first time I lived with Chris, I made some progress, but he did not know how far my life had fallen out of control. Eventually, I abused their goodwill, and he told me to leave.

The second time I stayed with Chris and Kelly, they knew my life was out of control and set firmer boundaries with me. I called Chris after being released unexpectedly from jail, and he dropped what he was doing to come and pick me up. Even with the experience of jail telling me to do something different, I was still unsure of who I was, and I eventually abused his goodwill again. He put me out again, as he should have.

Scott tried another tactic on his "help Ryan" journey. He made sure I knew my time in his condo was dependent on getting help, taking my GED, and maintaining a job. He risked his relationship with his roommate trying to help me. I attempted to fill his requirements but was lost. Toward the end of my stay with him, I walked in one day to find him kneeling by the couch with tears in his eyes. I didn't know it then but found out later he was crying out to Jesus to help me.

I couldn't see it then but recognize now that both my brothers tried to love me the best they knew how. They tried to point me toward what worked for them in life. None of us knew how confused I was as to who I was and where I was going.

One of the main tasks of recovery is taking a fearless and honest inventory of yourself—essentially, an assessment of life—and then filtering that through truth. You have to learn who you are in order to chart a path to a healthier version of yourself.

One of my favorite movies as a kid was *The NeverEnding Story*.[4] In it, the two main characters are on a journey, separately and together, toward a final confrontation of self. The main fantasy character Atreyu

---

4 *The NeverEnding Story*, directed by Wolfgang Peterson (1984; Warner Bros; Burbank, CA).

has to go through three magic gates in order to save the Childlike Empress from sickness and "the nothing," which is destroying everything in their world. The second gate he faces is a magic mirror, which reflects the true nature of the person. It is said that most men go screaming into the night when they see the truth of who they are. This is true for many in recovery as well. The third gate can only be trespassed by not wanting to trespass it, a paradox. Atreyu opens this gate by forgetting who he was and where he was going. The point being that to gain an understanding of identity, Atreyu must first face his reality then release his desires. In doing so, he finds what he is looking for in life.

I loved this movie consciously because of the story. Subconsciously, I think I wanted to know who I was as badly as Atreyu and Bastian, the two protagonists. I constantly reimagined myself in different lives and not just because of the drugs. I lived in a sea of identity outcomes that was as unrealistic as a world filled with luckdragons and a swamp of sadness. Heck, I lived in a swamp of sadness most days unless that day was peppered with chemicals and unrealistic fantasies about myself.

I didn't know it then, but Jesus was preparing to help me with this. I was on a crash course with myself some years still in the future. From a Christian recovery perspective, Jesus simultaneously complicates and simplifies the equation of identity. He tells us who we are to become, which makes identity formation easier, but His definition of who we are requires us to submit our own perception of self and desires for our future self, to Him. The irony is that by gaining our identity in Christ as He defines it, we do so by losing our identity forever. Sanctification is the process of looking more like Jesus and less like ourselves.

I have been crucified with Christ. It is no longer I who live, but Christ who lives in me. And the life I now live in the flesh I live by faith in the Son of God, who loved me and gave himself for me.

—Galatians 2:20

Chapter 7

DEATH

For years I was estranged from most of my family. I left home at eighteen after failing out of high school. Through my actions, I set off a nuclear bomb in the relationship I had with my father and stepmother. My two brothers wanted the best for me and individually took me into their homes on multiple occasions trying to help me find direction in life. I would predictably break their trust and violate their homes and boundaries. This resulted in more broken relationships and missed opportunities.

When I was out there in the world, I would periodically call my brothers, Scott and Chris, and tell them some half-truths about what I was doing and who I was at the time. Most of the time, I would at least partially believe my own lies. I was always about to go back to school. I was always starting a new promising job opportunity. I was always surrounding myself with positive people who were great influences on my life. I always had found the love of my life who was working to help me be the best version of me. In reality, I was always barely employed or not at all. I was always strung out on one substance or another with zero purpose in my life. I was always surrounded by other broken people looking for peace in all the wrong places.

Nevertheless, whenever I called, they would answer. They would listen to my stories and try to give me wisdom. I am sure they knew I was full of lies and would not have banked on anything I was saying as truth. Nevertheless, they would answer because they loved me in spite of my garbage.

In November 2002, I was floating from couch to couch trying to be as small as possible in people's lives so they would tolerate my eating their food and messing up the order of their lives and household. I was doing whatever I had to do to not sleep on the street, and I was at a particularly low spot in my journey. Sometimes, addiction leads us to believe that we are in control of the choices and outcomes of our lives, and at other times, we recognize that we are in a path of destruction. This was one of those latter seasons.

It was in the midst of this chaos that I made a truly random call to one of my brothers. God used this as a true moment of divine intervention.

My brother proceeded to inform me that my mother was most likely dying.

Since her brain injury in the late '80s, she had bounced from one assisted living facility to another. She spent most of that time in Pennsylvania near her only living sister. But just a few years earlier, my oldest brother Chris had become her Power of Attorney, and he moved her to a facility in Mecklenburg County, North Carolina, near where he lived. I never visited her once when she was there.

The day before this phone call, my mom had another heart attack and was on life support in the hospital. He informed me that if I was going to come that I needed to come now and in a hurry. I begged someone to buy me a bus ticket and got on a Greyhound bound for Charlotte.

When I got to the bus station in Charlotte, both of my sisters-in-law were there to take me to the hospital. I had on dirty clothes and smelled of stale cigarettes. I am sure they knew I was using. While their awareness of the direness of my own situation was clear, my mom's condition took precedent.

When I arrived at the hospital, I found myself entering the sterility of the Acute Coronary Care Unit of the hospital. My mom lay there intubated and on several machines. Within a day, the doctors told us that we had to make the decision whether to remove the machines and let nature take over. While there was a small chance she would have survived had we left her on the machines, it was clear that she would have been further impaired, and she had suffered enough in her condition. The doctor said that once the support was removed, she would only have a few minutes of life left in her used-up body. My brothers and I agreed, and quickly the staff came in and cut everything off. The beeps and groans of the machines that had become background noise were eliminated; instantly an eerie quiet settled into the room. All we could hear was her breath.

It took several hours for her to pass. We sat and watched as her heart rate and breathing went back and forth in an end-of-life death rhythm. Her breathing would slow as her heart raced to keep up. Then her breathing would increase as her heart would slow. During this time, a nurse would come in periodically and tell us to talk to her. The nurse said that she could hear us. I remember telling her that it was OK and for her to let go, but most of the time, we were silent. In her last moments this side of glory, we didn't know what to say.

Without warning, both her breathing and heart rate began to plummet. It was time. Scott's father-in-law, a longtime Presbyterian minister came into the room and recited Psalm 23, a psalm of David:

The LORD is my shepherd; I shall not want.
He makes me lie down in green pastures.
He leads me beside still waters.
He restores my soul.
He leads me in paths of righteousness for his name's sake.

Even though I walk through the valley of the shadow of death,
I will fear no evil, for you are with me;
your rod and your staff, they comfort me.
You prepare a table before me in the presence of my enemies;
you anoint my head with oil; my cup overflows.
Surely goodness and mercy shall follow me all the days of my life,
and I shall dwell in the house of the LORD forever.

As I believed myself definitionally agnostic, the experience of being at a deathbed with the Twenty-Third Psalm being recited by a reverend was completely surreal. While I didn't have any basis for understanding the Scripture, I understood that this was finality. As her life drained fully away from her body, I broke. For the first time since that morning in fifth grade, something inside me gave way; I wept uncontrollably for several hours. From the hospital room to my brother's house and as I lay down to sleep that night, I wept. Honestly, it was a cleansing experience.

The psalmist teaches us rest, comfort, hope, and encouragement through these six short verses. Ultimately, he shows us that true peace is found in the comfort and protection of a relationship with a loving God. At the time, I did not have the eyes to see or ears to hear that truth.

When she was lying there, gone, I noticed something that you only notice if you experience a death firsthand. One moment she was there; although she was hooked to machines, she was there. The minute she was deceased, her body was clearly a shell, not something altogether important. The critical element was gone . . . on to where, I had no idea at the time, but clearly gone. In my tears I knew that she wasn't confused, hurting, or scared any longer. Our body is simply a bag of bones that God uses as a vehicle for our soul. Once the soul is gone, the body, on this side of eternity, appears to be good for little to nothing.

The few days that passed between my arrival at the hospital and her death are mostly a blur, but with one distinct memory. One evening in the hospital, I was downstairs trying to find something to smoke. An addiction habit that I now see as disgusting is walking around to ash trays to locate other people's half smoked cigarettes. If that isn't a picture of a lost life, I don't know what is.

While engaged in my search, my siblings and their wives found me and did an impromptu intervention. They let me know that they knew that I was not doing well, and they wanted me to get some help. I remember sitting in a rocking chair as my sisters-in-law, Kelly and Sarah, listed programs that they thought I should go to—or at least ones they had found that appeared to be free. I know they listed three of four, but I was still consumed with myself and just told them what they wanted to hear in the moment. I told them I would think about it. I told them it wasn't as bad as they thought. They knew better.

What I didn't know is that soon God was going to use that conversation as a tool to change my life.

Over the coming days we held a memorial for Mom at a funeral home, and then it was time for everyone to go back to their regular lives. She was cremated, and there was no graveside service. Scott and Sarah drove me back to Greenville, and my dear brother tried to speak words of encouragement to me along the way.

As we neared Greenville, I began a pitch for him to give me a few dollars. I don't recall what my reasoning was, but I know my brother knew better than whatever line I was giving him. Because he loved me and didn't know what else to do, he gave me twenty or thirty dollars and dropped me off in a grocery store parking lot in downtown Greenville. He didn't want to, but I wouldn't let him know where I was staying. This is probably because I was unsure of where I was going to stay or what I would need to do to stay wherever that was. I cannot imagine how hard this was for him on the heels of losing his mother too. Dropping your brother off in the dark and cold of a November night in a grocery store parking lot is not something anyone should have to do. I immediately bought a pack of cigarettes and some booze and was back to the races.

When I walked back in the front door of my friend Jimmy's house, I was greeted, but I could see the shock on everyone's face. Had my mother not just died? Didn't I have somewhere else to go? Most importantly, the reality that they had been glad to be rid of me was evident. Not that they didn't care about me, but I was a cancer that wouldn't go away, and I was sleeping on their couch.

Although I didn't have a relationship with Mom at the time of her death, her absence reopened a wound uncovered only for a moment before I washed those emotions away with chemicals. Regardless of the reality that I had run from her existence in life and the truth that she didn't have the capacity to engage with me as a mother would anyway, I knew that she loved me and was my champion, even with her disabilities.

Back to the roller coaster of life I went with renewed fervor and focus. I chased peace at every turn finding its momentary counterfeit in the darkest parts of my created world.

Chapter 8

ASHES

It was only a few weeks after Mom died that I wound up back in jail with another set of charges for driving under the influence, driving under suspension, and a probation violation. While I don't remember much from that night, I apparently went up to a gas station around midnight in a friend's F-150 to get more alcohol. As soon as I got into the truck with the beer, I saw a police officer pull in beside me. I got back out of the truck with the intention of fooling the police officer by making a pretend phone call. Back then we still had phone booths at just about every gas station, so I walked over and picked up the phone like I was making a call. I thought I could outmaneuver him or wait him out.

Once the police officer went into the store, I got in the truck and headed out as quickly as I could. About a half mile down the road, I saw lights appear in my rearview mirror and I slammed my foot on the gas. I swerved into the apartment complex and into a parking spot about the same time that the blue lights caught up to me and skid in behind the truck.

When the officer got to my driver's side window, I simply said to him, "Would you let me finish my cigarette before you take me to jail."

I was drunk and illegally driving and knew I was caught. The officer was kind and let me light my cigarette before he placed me in cuffs.

Going to jail had become somewhat habitual at this point in life. I would run for a season, then spend the next season in county jail. I did this multiple times over countless years. If you have never been to jail, and consider that reality, I am sure it fills you with fear and anxiety. I can remember the first time I was incarcerated more than overnight when I was eighteen. It was scary and created all types of anxiety. Believe it or not, at this point in my journey I would say that going to jail was a relief.

Imagine a life that is filled with constant fear. Fear of the unknown as well as situational fear. After so many years of not having any stability in my life, and often not knowing where I was going to lay down my head or have my next meal, jail provided consistency and stability in a way that life just did not offer. Certainly, no one wants to be there, but I would bet that most people who have struggled with addiction and experienced homelessness would agree that jail, at times, provided a wonderful respite from the struggle to live. Once arrested, you spend the first half day in processing, which can be a long loud uncomfortable experience. For those who have relationships and resources, this is the point when they are calling their friends, relatives, and the bondsman. For the rest of us, we are waiting to get through this and be assigned to a cell.

No matter what city you are in, anywhere in the world, processing is mostly the same: searched, fingerprinted, photographed, stripped, and dressed out. Ultimately, you are given bedclothes and a bin and taken to your somewhat final destination. Each one of these tasks doesn't take a long time but there is often a lot of time in between them with no distraction. You are also typically in some type of holding cell that smells horrendously bad, like rotten teeth and corn chips. Ultimately, regardless of your wealth or ability to pay, you are waiting to see a judge for bond amount purposes.

You may not be familiar with the way the bond process works, so here's the short version. A judge assigns an amount and, in a relationship with a bondsman, you are typically responsible for ten to fifteen percent of the total price on the bond through a bondsman who signs for the total amount. Yes, that is right; a bond is a way for you to purchase your temporary freedom. The worse your crime, the higher the amount needed to sleep in your own bed.

For a petty criminal such as myself, the judge may assign a personal recognizance bond, meaning you sign yourself out agreeing to come back to court without having to put up cash or bond for your freedom. This is often the direction the judge takes to save the taxpayer from funding unnecessary incarcerations.

Another option is the judge assigns a piddly amount like $2,000. This would mean that you only need to come up with $200 to get a bondsman to sign you out. For someone in my situation, it really doesn't matter whether the bond is two million dollars or two hundred fifty dollars. When you're broke and have no one to call, the amounts do not matter.

In this instance, I was moved to a county detention center and assigned into an old-style cell with ten other men. The cell itself had beds for eight and the new guys were assigned a "sled," which is a plastic bed placed on the floor due to overcrowding.

There is for sure a pecking order in a jail cell, but so much depends on the population of inmates, why they are there, how long they have been there, and what consequence they are looking at. Sometimes, it is relationally easy, and sometimes it isn't. In this case it was easy. I got into a real bed within a few days, and I settled into a routine.

4:00 a.m.	Wake up
4:10 a.m.	Eat
11:00 a.m.	Eat
4:00 p.m.	Eat
8:00 p.m.	Sleep

The times between eating were used to tell lies, brag about lies, play cards, read, dwell on the past, and tell more lies. Years earlier, on a short bid in a county jail, I had begun writing poetry to pass the time. When incarcerated, I often wrote more than usual because I didn't have anything else to do.

Here is a poem I wrote in jail in 2002 to describe the experience and my mental frame of mind in the moment:

A hollow clank on plastic glass, the echo of closed doors
A metal frame that is my bed, the cold of concrete floors
A sheet that ties instead of grips, a mattress made of foam
I put an X upon this date, marks another day at home
These clothes the color of fire stay, upon this body for a week
Till I'm allowed to change them out, this future seems so bleak
My mind it wanders endlessly through open corridors
In passages that twist and turn and lead to dead end doors
A key is what I yearn to find to get out of this hole
Not made of copper, gold, or brass but needed to make me whole

During these months I would write to people as well. I would typically write to a few friends as well as my brothers to let them know where I was and what I was doing. Selfishly, I also wanted them to put some money on my canteen fund so I could buy some ramen noodles and honey buns. These letters would be filled with earnest desires to straighten up and fly right, but each of the recipients also knew that I didn't have the follow-through or gumption to do something different. Good intentions will only get you so far in life and as the well-known proverb says, "The road to hell is paved with good intentions."

I never had many visitors. I think that of all the times I was in jail, I received three or four visits. This time, I got an unexpected visit from my middle brother, Scott. Movies and TV shows actually do justice to the visitation experience. Depending on the jail, there is typically some type of room separated from another room by a plexiglass partition. Some rooms have phones to use; some just have holes drilled in the plexiglass that you have to scream through to be heard. None of the rooms are private; all appear sterile and old, and everything is loud.

Scott entered the visitation room and looked nervous. I would assume that he had never been in a jail before and probably hasn't been in one since. Additionally, he was visiting his baby brother who was out of control and had been for a long time. Here we were, face to face. Me in my orange jumpsuit, unshaven and unkempt and my brother in his stability of life.

I cannot recall what we talked about at first. He was recently married but without kids at this point. We did not have anything in common other than our blood, and it was a strange and scary situation for him.

He then proceeded to tell me that he, my older brother Chris, and their wives, were driving to Long Island, New York, to spread my mother's ashes at Jones Beach, which was her childhood beach. I was instantaneously furious, and he knew it. I begged him to wait for me to get out, and he said no. All these years later, I have made peace with the decision, but in the moment, I don't recall that I had ever felt more abandoned, ostracized, alone, and angry. In fairness, I had not had much contact with my mother in the years preceding her death, nor had I had much contact with any of them. I was a ghost to my family, but I felt so betrayed. I couldn't articulate it then, but I saw that as an opportunity for closure, and I perceived I was being robbed of the opportunity. She was my mom too, and I didn't have a voice in the decision; even her ashes disappeared from my life.

As much as it hurt, I can now see that they made the right decision. I was an outlier and not worthy of consideration for major decisions. They also were after closure on this chapter of their lives, and they were the adults who were stable enough to go after it. I don't remember what I said to Scott, but I am sure it was filled with tears and fury. I imagine that his drive home was hard that day. I was a caged animal unable to process my emotions, so I had done what I always did and vomited my emotions all over someone who cared deeply for me. Through the years, my brothers had lots of experiences where they had to leave me physically or verbally—times when they left sad and disappointed.

I remember lying down in my bunk that night and thinking, *"Where was God in all this? Where was He, and why was my life turning out this way? Why was I so broken? Why couldn't I change?"*

It would be years before I truly understood that God was using all this for my good and His glory. It would be more years before I could process my mother's illness, life, and death. Some people buy into a false hope that when you get clean and trust in Jesus, all the issues and garbage go away. They think that if they walk down an aisle and make some proclamation, all will be better.

The short answer is that it will. The longer answer is that it will but not in the way that you think. Following Jesus is a lifelong commitment, and the Bible never promises an easy life. On the contrary, the Bible promises hardship and trials. The bonus is that those hardships and trials are accompanied by joy and peace, neither of which is dependent on the way we feel. The bonus to the bonus is that you don't have to do those things alone; Jesus is always with you.

It has been decades since my mom died, almost forty years since she got sick, and over twenty years since her ashes were spread by my brothers on a random day nearly a thousand miles from where I sit now. Today, that wound is continuing to heal, but I don't think it will ever be healed completely, and I don't think it is supposed to be. Today, I can live my life and trust that Jesus has my back. I certainly do not always cry when I see something that reminds me of her. But sometimes I cry. I still miss her every day that I remember her, and today, I don't think I ever want to get to a place where I don't.

As I mentioned before, a few years ago I realized that I couldn't remember her voice anymore. I try to conjure it in my mind and no matter how hard I concentrate or how quiet the room gets, I can't find it. Honestly, I find it hard to remember much about her except for the few pictures that I have and some memories. I am not sure whether these memories are mine or just stories I have been told a thousand times.

When I randomly feel the sting of loss, I am reminded of her and of my humanity. No matter how much success I find in life, I am still a little boy who misses his mom. I don't want to ever lose that.

God's grace helps me with this dilemma. He allowed me to process my grief and work through my issues, and He still does to this day. More than that, and because He can, he provided me with an amazing wife who loves our children the way I remember my mom loving me. I see my mom in Lauren in so many ways, and now I see my mom in my own kids. The way they love animals, and the way they love me reminds me of the fierce love my mother had for me in the years I was blessed to have with her.

Chapter 9

PROVIDENCE

Eventually, I finished serving my time and was released from jail. The same flood of relief that I felt coming into jail disappeared the minute I was out and understood that I literally had nowhere to go. I had been corresponding with some friends from jail and one of my dearest friends, Kristen, offered me a place to live in Charleston, South Carolina. The problem was that I had to get from the Upstate of South Carolina to the coast.

I called another lifelong friend, Chris, and he immediately dropped what he was doing and picked me up from the sidewalk outside the clink. I only spent a few days with Chris before I secured transport to Charleston and off, I went. At this point I was committed to not drinking or drugging anymore. I believe I made that commitment every time that I was released from jail but would quickly violate my own commitment. I mean it was laughable, really. I was committed until I was offered the first opportunity to drink or drug. This time would be no different.

People struggling with addiction will commonly try a geographical shift. The thought is: *"If I just move somewhere else, then I won't have any of these problems; no one will know me, and I can start fresh."* The problem is that wherever you go, there you are. We are always our own worst enemies.

For years I heard my parents and others talk about being concerned about the "crowd" I was hanging out with. Essentially, this was taking the blame for our problems and decisions and putting it on some external force or person that is supposedly causing us to do the things we do and be the person we are.

Years later, I would realize that I was the bad guy; I was the wrong crowd. I was the person whom other parents should warn their kids away from. Time has a way of sifting our truth and showing us who we really are. Eventually, all the bad people have bad outcomes, and all the better people have better outcomes. If my outcomes were any reflection of the truth of my heart, I was very bad indeed. During this same moment of realization, I understood one of the only pieces of wisdom I can articulate that I think is an original thought: *"All the people I thought were the cool kids in high school were really all the losers, and all the kids I thought were losers were really the cool kids."*

The really cool kids were the ones who in their early twenties were finishing college, starting careers, and had their own life trajectory; often they were in the process of purchasing their first homes. They had great relationships with their friends and families and thought of someone other than themselves most of the time. Unfortunately, this honesty was still a long way from the surface, and I was still 100 percent self-centered, and my identity was completely fractured. I was still whoever I needed to be to survive.

After I got to Charleston, I made it less than a couple of hours before I was drinking and only a few days before I was smoking weed. A note to those that are still struggling with addiction: a geographical move to a college beach town is a bad idea.

I quickly found employment but that only served to extend the amount of time for me to reach a bottom. Over the course of the next month I worked, drank, and partied. I slipped deeper and deeper into drinking and drugs. I slipped deeper into depression and self-hatred. I was heading toward a collision with God, and I did not know it was over a near horizon.

Depression and addiction go hand in hand. For me they were inseparable like green and grass. Every time I found myself losing control of my drinking and drug use, I also found myself feeling more and more hopeless and depressed. Guess what seemed like the only antidote to that depression—drinking and drug use, of course. To me, this was the cycle of addiction as I knew it. Anxiety and depression seep into every crevice of existence. When engaged, it infiltrates every fiber of your being, like angry bees swarming around your head that you cannot see or swat. As soon as you realize you are awake, anxiety returns like a flood. It makes you terrified and nauseous and emotional. It feels like there is a giant creature around every corner about to eat you. Take a big gulp from a bottle of vodka during that experience, and it is like someone shuts off the fire hydrant of fear. For a moment, everything returns to normal, or at least what passes for normal. For a moment, you are at peace.

Much like being in the eye of a storm, peace was fleeting and only found in the bottom of a bottle or an empty bag of dope. Counterfeit peace gives a false sense of calm in an otherwise raging and chaotic existence. Every second of counterfeit peace had a storm raging all around it.

When I eventually met Jesus, I truly met the Prince of Peace.

And a great windstorm arose, and the waves were breaking into the boat, so that the boat was already filling. But he was in the stern, asleep on the cushion. And they woke him and said to him, "Teacher, do you not care that we are perishing?" And he awoke and rebuked the wind and said to the sea, "Peace! Be still!" And the wind ceased, and there was a great calm. He said to them, "Why are you so afraid? Have you still no faith?" And they were filled with great fear and

said to one another, "Who then is this, that even the wind
and the sea obey him?"
—Mark 4:37–41

There are a lot of things that people go to for peace in this world, but I am telling you that for me there is nothing like Jesus. He isn't peace in the eye of the storm; He is peace that comes regardless of the storm. The storm might be screaming in every direction, and Jesus just sits back and takes a nap. If we trust in Him, we get to take a nap too.

Again, I didn't know Him; I didn't know any resource on the planet to eliminate the storm of life other than drinking and drug use, and they were killing me. At first, they were doing it slowly and so quietly that I did not perceive it, but much like a storm, the barometric pressure was dropping, and a front had moved in.

Suicide is an abnormal thing for someone to think about, but when you are caught in a never-ending cycle of destruction with no way to stop the tidal wave of emotions and fear, suicide can seem like a logical step toward final peace. Where drinking might bring temporary peace, death would be permanent peace, eliminating the storm from returning. I am grateful that most of you cannot fathom the idea of thinking of your own death, but for some of us, suicide is not a random thought but an obsession. In the moment, the suicidal person rationalizes that this single choice has the power to bring eternal peace.

I first attempted suicide as a kid. I do not remember how old I was, but I know it was after my mother's illness and the divorce, and I don't think it was a valid attempt as much as an experimentation. I remember fashioning a noose out of a cord of rope and hooking it and myself to a pullup bar hanging in the doorway of my brother's room. I held myself under the bar and eventually let go. As quickly as I felt the rope tighten, I panicked and grabbed the bar. Thankfully, I was able to remove the rope from my neck before my arms gave out. The experience was terrifying, and I didn't have another thought like that for a long time.

The second time I attempted suicide, I cut my wrists open. I think I was eighteen; I was living with a man and his wife in a very rough neighborhood in west Greenville. None of my friends and family were talking to me, and I was working at an oil change shop. I do not believe that any specific event precipitated my attempt other than my being sad and lost. I wound up at a hospital and was quickly released. I think with that attempt, I went from experimentation to a cry for help. I wanted someone to truly see me, see the pain in my heart as my blood ran red out of my body. At the hospital I had buyer's remorse and quickly tried to convince the doctors that this was a mistake. I wanted my family back, not a straitjacket.

The third time that I attempted suicide, I was around nineteen or twenty years old. I was homeless and living on a friend's couch, and I had worn out my welcome again. I knew that David would have to ask me to leave in the next few days, and I was lost as to what to do. So, I rationalized that suicide was a way to escape the cacophony of voices in my head.

This attempt was legitimate. I got drunk and sat down in David's bathroom. I picked up the razor and cut each wrist in two directions— essentially and ironically, cutting a cross. This wasn't done for any religious reasons, but rather because I was confused as to what the right direction was. As I watched the blood drain, I panicked again. I did not want to die, but I did not know what to do. I really don't remember specifics, but I believe I called David's girlfriend, Summer, and they drove over and found me passed out, covered in my own blood in the tub. EMS took me to the hospital and within a day, I had again convinced the hospital staff to release me.

While in the hospital I convinced a young nurse to take me outside for a cigarette. Because I had been admitted for a suicide attempt, she couldn't leave me alone, and we struck up a conversation. She couldn't fathom why I did what I did, and I couldn't fathom how her life was so normal. She had gone the normal route in life, completed college, and was starting out strong in her independence. I was a dope addict who cared about having a cigarette despite having fresh stitches in my wrists.

Now while these were legitimate suicide attempts, there are dozens of other moments that I did things that were suicidal in nature but not valid attempts. I played Russian Roulette more than once. I walked on the edges of the tops of buildings. I took more drugs than were safe to ingest. I generally got to a place where I was flippant about life. Life without Jesus was completely empty and void of purpose. The only way to counter fear and loneliness was to live in the extremes.

In Charleston, depression and addiction had again built to a boiling point. I had begun to obsess and fanaticize about my own death, again. Where would I get a gun? Should I cut my leg at my femoral artery? Where can I get enough pills to do the job?

Even in this insanity I did not want to die. I wanted to live, but I didn't know how. I desperately wanted to find true peace and was beginning to see that the avenues that I was using provided only fool's gold. While I didn't know the real thing, I was starting to see the peace I was pursuing as the counterfeit that it was. In the midst of these realizations, I was torn apart daily by these two insistent voices in my head: "Live." "Die."

I asked my friend, Albert, to pick me up and we drove to a rock jetty behind The Citadel. Even with the conflicting voices, I had come up with a plan that I thought was perfect. I would swim out into the ocean until I was far enough and tired enough that I couldn't make it back in. My arms and legs would fail me, and I would drown, probably never to be seen again. I would just disappear. I mean I already felt like I had disappeared. This would just complete the task.

As we sat there drinking Colt 45s on those rocks, I confessed to Albert what I was thinking. I confessed that I didn't want to die, and I didn't want to live. I confessed that I knew all the roads to peace in my life dead-ended at sheer cliffs. The duality of the thoughts was definitional insanity in my life, and something had to give. Albert and I were not close enough for me to lay this on him, but he was, and I am sure still is, a kind soul, and he did the most important thing in the world during this moment: he listened.

He didn't try to comfort me or fix me or correct me. He listened and at the right moment, he asked one question: "If you decide to live, where would you get help?" I don't know whether you remember the moment in the hospital, as my mother lay dying, when my brothers and my sweet sisters-in-law tried to have an intervention. Sitting on the rocks staring out into Charleston Bay, I could only remember the name of one place I could get help, Miracle Hill Ministries.

I had never been to Miracle Hill. I didn't even know what it was. All I knew was that it existed in the Upstate of South Carolina and that it had a program for people like me. Albert talked me off the rocks and into his car. Over the next twenty-four hours, I made my way to Greenville and into the front doors of the Greenville Rescue Mission. God was on the move in my life, and I didn't know it.

Isn't that always the case? During the moments when the Lord is active, we often do not see it. We are surrounded by the storm and the noise, and we can't see two feet in front of us. The series of events that had led me to this moment seemed unrelated and random at the time, but they were part of God's providence in my life. We often ask ourselves, "what if" when a situation works out a certain way. That's a bad question on its face. God has us where He wants us. We work to run from Him, and He is circling around us on the other side. How was I supposed to know that God would ultimately use an internet search done by one of my sisters-in-law to shift my life so dramatically?

Chapter 10

OVERCOMERS

Within a day, I was walking into the front door of a Miracle Hill Ministries shelter, the Greenville Rescue Mission, scared to death, not about my location but about my life. The first person I met at the Rescue Mission was Curtis Pitts. Curtis was built to help men with addiction issues. After a lifetime of service in state-level programs and legal circles, he had moved over to Miracle Hill, as he desired to live out his faith in his career and help others. When I arrived, he had been the director of the Overcomers Program for a few months and was working to incorporate sound recovery principles into a program already thick with biblical teaching. Overcomers is a seven-month Christ-Centered discipleship program focused on helping men with life-dominating issues. This is a fancy way of saying it's a Christian recovery program. For my purposes, it was rehab.

It is important to note that at this point in my life, I was not an atheist. My thoughts and beliefs were clearly those of a skeptic, a doubter, and a scoffer. I thought that God was undefinable. I believed that there was a god, but I was convinced that whoever or whatever god was, it hated me. I thought I was simply an ant on the planet and that God was a little kid playing with a magnifying glass, burning me up for fun. On top of this theory, I had a real dislike of all things Christian. You might even say that I had some strong apologetics against Jesus, but I was desperate and willing to do anything or be anywhere that offered help.

I do not remember the whole conversation that Curtis and I had that day, but I could tell he was a kind man, and he knew that I was broken. The only question I remember him asking me is the same question I have heard him ask hundreds of men after me—the same question I have asked thousands of men myself: What are you willing to do to change your life?

The answer for me was the answer that he was looking for: anything. Unfortunately, I was too strung out to even get into the program because Miracle Hill is set up for life change and as such is not a medical program. This means that if there is a chance that someone will go into withdrawal from lack of use, they first need to be seen medically.

I spent my first night at the Rescue Mission in A-dorm, which is the starting dorm on the shelter side of the building. I had to spend the night there and wait to check into detox the following day. You might think that checking into a shelter would be a scary experience, and for some I am sure that it is. But I had checked into numerous city and county jails and was relieved to be in a safe place, even if I had twenty-nine roommates in the dorm.

The next day I was sent to detox, and I spent four or five days there before I returned to check into Overcomers officially. Upon return to the Rescue Mission, I was faced with the stark reality not only of life in a mission but also in a structured program. Up to this point I had spent time in jails, detox facilities, a state-run program, and hospitals, but they were all forced upon me. This was the first time I had been anywhere by choice. Acclimating to the program was surprisingly easy. Once you are used to institutional living, it does not matter what the institution is or how it operates. Even so, every institution has its own culture, and Overcomers was no different in that regard.

If you are an outsider looking into a mission or a program, you might see a lot of individuals who are doing the right thing and staying in line with the institution's rules and policies. Most of those individuals know how to play the game; they are experts in going along to get along. For a longer program like Overcomers, the dorms are filled with master manipulators who not only know how to play the game but have mastered the art of deception. I was no different.

The program was set up in such a way that each guest spends about half their day in classes, and they spend the other half doing tasks in the building. The classes cover anything from relapse prevention to journaling lessons and everything in between. For the first time in my memory, I was hungry to learn. I was starving for direction, and I found it at Overcomers. I found myself craving knowledge and self-exploration like I never had before, and I gobbled up everything that the counselors threw at me. One counselor, Rick Scholette, took me under his wing and started giving me extra assignments. I did those as well.

I tell people all the time that you do not have to be a believer to be at Miracle Hill, but you are going to hear an awful lot about Jesus while you are there. This was true of Overcomers then and now. Most of the classes and assignments have a Christian and biblical worldview attached to them, and this portion of the curriculum was very hard for me to digest. A starving man will eat just about anything to survive, and my hunger was greater than my dislike of the materials. I ate up everything.

Months into the program, as the fog of my brain started fading away, I found myself wrestling with the Lord for the first time in my life. The counselors would suggest some truth, and I would try to knock holes in it. A chapel speaker would preach on some issue, and I would try to determine whether the world had greater wisdom.

I began reading everything that I could lay my hands on. I haven't covered this yet, but I have been a voracious reader my whole life. My mom and oldest brother contributed to that desire. Ever since I can remember, I always have had a book nearby; most of the time, reading additionally served as an escape mechanism.

The books I read at Overcomers had the opposite effect. Instead of escaping into a book, I was coming alive in the books. I read every major book on theology I could find. I read the Bible and then reread the Bible, attempting to find flaws. I read books on purpose and drive, history, and psychology. When I wasn't in class, working on a task, or playing volleyball with the guys, I was reading.

It was like my life was a puzzle and I thought somewhere in the books lay the directions on how to decipher the broken pieces and put them together. That is hard to do when you can't see what is on the individual puzzle pieces. Gradually, the classes and books began to give definition to who I was and what made me tick.

While the staff might have found it hard to figure out who was serious about the program and life change, the guests often know who is playing the game and who isn't. Remember that the building is full of master manipulators, and they can smell each other out. If you are serious about change, you wind up alienating most of your peers. I found my circle of friends getting smaller, but much more intimate. I have never been to war or served in the military, but from talking to others who have, I believe that a war zone drives fellow soldiers into a very intimate relationship with one another. They are fighting for their lives together and must count on the man beside them. I believe the same thing happens to men who are earnestly trying to change their lives together. They too are fighting for their lives in a very different way, and they are spilling blood along the way. I have found some of my closest friendships in the trenches of a recovery program. Some of those relationships can be separated by miles, years, and decisions, but we remain close because of the shared bond of struggle.

Maybe the most amazing aspect of those early months of recovery was that I was experiencing peace, even if I was blind to it in the moment. For the first time in my adult life, I was not using anything to eliminate the chaos of my life and yet my life was quiet. I went to sleep easily and woke up early, not worried about the day. The counterfeit peace was removed, replaced with contentment as I was on the cusp of finding true healing in my life.

Curtis asked a question about life change in the same way that Naaman is asked about life change in 2 Kings chapter 5. Naaman is the commander of the army of Syria, and he suffers from leprosy. Through a providential series of events, he finds himself pursuing healing from Elisha. Elisha sends a message to him, telling him to wash himself in the Jordan seven times to be healed. Naaman, a proud man, angrily says:

> *Are not Abana and Pharpar, the rivers of Damascus, better than all the waters of Israel? Could I not wash in them and be clean?" So he turned and went away in a rage.*
> —2 Kings 5:12

To Naaman the requirements of healing were too much to handle. In his mind the Jordan was a river below his standard and outside his comfort and experience. For all he knew, it was used by people to water their animals and filled with sewage and trash. He believed it was beneath him to do this thing that Elisha was suggesting. Through a moment of humility, Naaman listens to his servants, of all people, dips himself in the Jordan, and on the seventh dip, *"his flesh was restored like the flesh of a little child, and he was clean"* (2 Kings 5:14).

I learned this Bible lesson from another great counselor, Mark Alverson (aka Uncle Mark), years later. In a sense God is asking each of us, "What are you willing to do to change your life?" For me, the answer was clear; I was willing to do anything.

I would have dipped myself a hundred times in raw sewage to not feel the way I felt and live the results that I had earned in life. To allow change to happen in our lives, we must be open to God's leading, submissive, and obedient. Some of us are not struggling with addiction and brokenness the way our guests do in our shelters and programs each day, but each of us has some form of leprosy. I have found that more times than not, our healing is waiting for us under "filthy waters" or doing something we do not want to do. I think many people go through their whole lives not addressing their brokenness because their pride will not allow them to listen to the still small voice of God telling them to take a swim.

The amazing part of the passage is not that Naaman finds healing in the waters but that his restoration takes him beyond his broken places and restores him to his youth. Not only are his leprous growths removed, but possibly every scar from every battle he had ever been in is also healed. When God is in the life-change equation, watch out. He will take you further than you can imagine and fix things you did not even know were broken.

Chapter 11

SALVATION

My Days at the Rescue Mission passed quickly. I slowly worked my way toward emotional, mental, and physical health, or the closest I had been to those definitions in my life. I was assigned different tasks depending on what level of the program I was in, but I slowly jockeyed for position and found myself working at the CID (Client Information Desk). This was a prime job because you got to sit around all day, and you essentially had the keys to the kingdom. The magnetically locked front door that every guest passes through is controlled out of this office, and everyone must go through you to see a staff member, get a pass, or get back into the building. The other benefits were that you were allowed to interact with the staff at a greater level and given access to a coffee maker.

In those days, the Rescue Mission operated two related but very different ministries out of the building. One side of the building was devoted to Overcomers, and the other side was for mission guests, those who were experiencing homelessness but not committed to a long-term addiction recovery program. The relationship between the two populations was often counterproductive and created or exacerbated relational issues and poor decision-making, ultimately resulting in

Overcomers moving to its own facility some years later. There was continual friction between the two populations because of the perceived differences in their motives for being there, but in reality, there is no difference between the groups. Both groups are homeless men who needed help but had different commitment levels; sometimes, they were often their own worst enemies. In fact, Miracle Hill's programs were designed to help the shelter population. There are a few common issues found in the population of those experiencing homelessness, addiction being near the top of the list.

As an Overcomer client, you would not normally have a lot of contact with the mission staff unless you worked on a task that brought you into proximity with them. I was lucky enough to be one of those individuals and found a whole new source of wisdom to drink from daily.

One of the mission staff members was a man named Bill Slocum. Bill and his wife Janine both worked for Miracle Hill; Bill could not have been more different from me, or so I thought. He was twenty-five years older than me, highly educated, and had worked in churches and ministry longer than I had been alive. He seemed to genuinely care about me for no reason, and he would stop by the CID daily for a chat and to see how I was doing.

Bill and I have now been friends for decades, and I know that this is not naturally the way that he is built. He is an introvert, like me, and is happy to not engage for days at a time. However, Jesus had been working on Bill for a very long time and had created a deep longing for relationship and connection.

Not every week, but regularly, Bill would check on me and ask me how the program was going. Often, he would probe as to what I was learning about the Bible, and I learned that he wasn't scared of my hard questions. I would regularly ask him questions about his God:

- Why are there sixty-six books instead of seventy or fifty-five?
- Why do bad things happen to good people?
- Why would God allow me to be an addict if he loves me?

- Why can't we talk to God like Moses did?
- Why should I trust a book written by someone else about a God I can't see?

Bill wasn't scared of my questions and even though some of my questions were ridiculous, he would pause, think, and then patiently give me an answer that I could understand. Bill was aware of my appetite for books and would often inquire what I thought about this book or that book. He would chime in with his own thoughts from time to time. Eventually, he began asking about my family relationships and after I explained that I really didn't have a family member who wanted anything to do with me, he let me know that he and others cared about me. I believed him. Curtis, Bill, and the other staff members were teaching me something about relationships. They were loving me even though I thought I was unlovable. They didn't tell me they loved me; they showed me they loved me in every interaction, and I grew to love them too.

Most importantly, they were teaching me how God loves us. I knew that there was not anything redeemable about my life from the world's perspective, but they loved me anyway. Years later in a mentor training session, I heard another staff member, Ken Kelly, quote Zig Ziglar as saying, "People don't care how much you know until they know how much you care."[1]

In my opinion this statement is filled with truth and is one of the most important principles someone who desires to work in ministry should understand. If we want to influence someone's life in a positive way, then they first must understand in their bones that we care for them. It can't be lip service. I disregarded so many chapel speakers back then because they would preach from a position of us versus them, and they would scream at me about how I needed to fix my life. This had zero

---

1   Zig Ziglar, Goodreads, https://www.goodreads.com/quotes/863418-people-don-t-care-how-much-you-know-until-they-know.

effect on me. I knew my life was a mess and did not need some stranger telling me so. I certainly did not trust a man who spent thirty minutes elevating himself as better than me to tell me I was broken and in need of repair.

What I needed and found at the Rescue Mission was a handful of men who were willing to get down in the muck and mire of my life and wade around in it. They were not scared of the stench or the scenery, and they did it with earnest smiles on their faces. Bill not only became one of my favorite people on the planet, but he became a true ambassador of Christ in my life. So did Curtis. So did Rick. So did Allen. So did Randy. And dozens of other amazing men and women of the faith over the years.

One day, months into my relationship with Bill, he stopped by CID and nonchalantly dropped off a book, *More Than a Carpenter* by Josh McDowell. Up to this point I had read much more challenging books about Christianity. I had read textbooks on theology. I had read commentaries, and parables, and apologetics books; I even kept a copy of *The Moody Handbook on Theology* in my locker. This copy of *More Than a Carpenter* that Bill laid on the desk was tiny, not 150 pages, and simply written. I trusted Bill and since he gave it to me, I would read it.

I believe this was a Friday and I headed into the weekend with dreams of volleyball, trips to the canteen, and movie night. That evening, I started reading *More Than a Carpenter* before dinner. After dinner I picked the book up and started reading again. In chapter two McDowell lays out C. S. Lewis's argument that Jesus must be viewed as either a liar, lunatic, or Lord.[2] The argument is that Jesus has to be one of these three options because he claimed to be God. He was either a liar who knew that he wasn't God and was making it up, or he was a lunatic who thought he was God but wasn't. The last and most absurd option is that He was in fact God.

---

2 Josh McDowell, *More Than a Carpenter* (Wheaton, IL: Tyndale House Publishers, 1977), 22–35.

Chapter 5 is all about the disciples. It is titled, "Who Would Die for a Lie?" Essentially McDowell's argument is that if anyone knew the answer to C. S. Lewis's question, it was the disciples. These guys spent three years with the man and knew everything about Him. If He was a liar, they knew it and were in on the charade. If He were a lunatic, they would have been complicit in His psychosis and manipulation of the people. If the "miracles" were hogwash, they would have been the henchmen behind the scenes hiding the loaves and fishes from view.[3] While reading I realized that the disciples were just normal guys like me. They were fishermen, a tax collector, a political operative, a thief, and the others held a variety of other normal everyday jobs.

So, what do the disciples do when Jesus is arrested? They run away. They have a completely normal reaction to the party ending in their pursuit of self-preservation. Then in the story, Jesus supposedly rises from the dead. Their response to His resurrection unlocked something deep in my soul. As a response to His resurrection, they chose—*chose* being the key word—to die as martyrs. When they interact with the risen Savior, most wind up in situations where they must choose to deny Christ or die. Six are crucified. Matthew dies by the sword. Thaddaeus is killed by arrows. His brother is stoned to death, and Thomas takes a spear to the chest.

I have done a lot of wild things in my life, but I knew that I would not die for another man's lunacy or lie. I might lie with him for a while, but I am not choosing to be crucified upside down on his account like Peter. The man who denied Jesus three times chose suffering over denial in the end.

As I reflected, I thought of the book of James, which I had just learned was written by Jesus's half-brother. I have two brothers and realized that if one of them told me he was God, I would be challenged to know whether to laugh in his face or call the men in the white coats. Clearly, if anyone knew whether Jesus was legit, it was his brother. James,

---

3 McDowell, 60–71.

like the twelve disciples before him, chose death, and was martyred by the pharisees on the order of the high priest Ananus Ben Ananus. He chose to be stoned to death or thrown from a tower, depending on which historian you believe—no one would take either choice to die for a lie.

This was the breaking point for me; normal men would not systematically choose death to maintain another man's lies or lunacy. For months I had wrestled with God. For months I had fought off every attempt to tear down the walls around my heart, and God used the final testimony of faith of these men to show me who He was.

In that moment I saw the men God had put around me and their love for me in a new light. They were daily laying down their lives, choosing a path of service rather than money, all in the name of Jesus. In this moment I saw the absurd level of love that God has for me.

Looking to Jesus, the founder and perfecter of our faith, who for the joy that was set before Him endured the cross, despising the shame, and is seated at the right hand of the throne of God.

—Hebrews 12:2

Jesus had in fact died for my sins. What a fool I had been to think anything other than this eternal truth. In an instant the veil really was pulled from my eyes, and I saw clearly for the first time in my life.

Silently, but filled with joy and emotion, I grabbed my buddy Shane and walked down to the chapel. The room was empty except for the two of us, and I prayed a sinner's prayer. That was July 18, 2003.

If I am telling this story in front of a church congregation, this is the point when I would get a round of applause from the audience. In truth, I think I was saved thirty minutes earlier when I hit the breaking point on page 61 of *More Than a Carpenter*. It was then that I knew Jesus was who He said He was. It was in that moment that I realized I was a sinner in need of a savior, and I believe it was in that moment, through my tears, something moved in my spirit, and I invited Jesus to be both Lord and Savior of my life.

The words I spoke in that chapel were a powerful exclamation point to the moment I accepted and invited Jesus into my life, but they held no supernatural power. The mystery happened in the months leading up to this point as God shifted the foundation of my reality.

That Monday the two people that I wanted to tell more than anyone in the world were Curtis and Bill. These spiritual giants were now my brothers, and I could not wait to share with them how Jesus my Savior had moved in my life.

Chapter 12

F BOMBS

All these years later I am still blown away that God would choose to save a sinner like me. I am being careful not to get into the details of how far my life had spiraled out of control, but it was as bad as you allow your imagination to go. I think Romans 1 sums it up pretty well.

> *And since they did not see fit to acknowledge God, God gave them up to a debased mind to do what ought not to be done. They were filled with all manner of unrighteousness, evil, covetousness, malice. They are full of envy, murder, strife, deceit, maliciousness. They are gossips, slanderers, haters of God, insolent, haughty, boastful, inventors of evil, disobedient to parents, foolish, faithless, heartless, ruthless.*
> —Romans 1:28–31

Once I knew Jesus, the lessons I was learning started to come to life in a new way, and I dove deeper into the Scriptures. When we are in a situation where our life is changing, I think it is hard to see the change in real time. It is like losing weight and not being able to see any significant change in the mirror but looking back at an old picture and going, oh.

Some months after I met Jesus, I had a dentist appointment with a local free dental clinic. Specifically, I was going to have two of my wisdom teeth taken out; something that should have been done years before.

I was sitting in the waiting room waiting for my name to be called when a couple of new people walked in, checked in, and had a seat. These people were louder than what was probably appropriate, and it wasn't long until I heard one of them drop an f-bomb—the king of the curse words.

The weird part was that I **heard** the word. I had spoken like a sailor for as long as I could remember and had said that word more times than I can count. I had lived in a world where that word was as common as the word *the* in most sentences. For the first time since I was a child the word sounded rough in my ears and soul like sandpaper. It sounded harsh and wrong and, well, like a curse. I almost felt like a kid getting ready to be caught for something, as if I was hiding in a closet with a stolen box of cookies. It was as if I had said the word, not just heard it.

In Overcomers we were taught a lot about Ephesians 6 and the armor of God:

> *Put on the whole armor of God, that you may be able to stand against the schemes of the devil. For we do not wrestle against flesh and blood, but against the rulers, against the authorities, against the cosmic powers over this present darkness, against the spiritual forces of evil in the heavenly places. Therefore take up the whole armor of God, that you may be able to withstand in the evil day, and having done all, to stand firm.*
>
> —Ephesians 6:11–13

Having heard so many lessons on the subject, I think that I believed it to be more poetic than anything else. Yeah, yeah, yeah, I need to put on my belt of truth; yeah, yeah, yeah, I know the word is my sword.

Eventually, they called me back to see the dentist, and I got my wisdom teeth out the old-fashioned way, brute force sans Novocain. That is how it is done if it is done at a free clinic. That night as I was getting ready for bed and icing my swollen cheek, I kept reflecting on what had happened that afternoon and wrestling with what exactly was different from every other time I had heard or said the word. Sure, it was against the rules to curse at Overcomers, but was it simply absence of the word that made it sound so hard?

Eventually, I hit upon the understanding that as God had been softening my heart and as I was clinging to the hem of His robe, He was sanctifying me. He was cleaning out all the garbage in my heart, soul, and body and replacing it with something new. Over all those years of hard living, I had built up callouses to the world and all things worldly.

For this people's heart has become calloused; they hardly hear with their ears, and they have closed their eyes. Otherwise they might see with their eyes, hear with their ears, understand with their hearts and turn, and I would heal them.

—Matthew 13:15 NIV

I remember one time when I was living in Charlotte in a townhouse by myself, I heard a knock at the door. When I looked through the keyhole, I saw the telltale signs that they probably were either Mormons or Jehovah's Witnesses come to save my soul. I looked around at the pornography playing on the TV, the empty bottles of beer on the table surrounded by random drug paraphernalia, and I smelled the pungent odor of marijuana in the air. I looked crazy to the world, and my living situation was a clear reflection of the status of my heart.

I opened the door and invited the two young men in just to see what they would do under the circumstances. Frankly, I thought it would be amusing to see them squirm. To their credit, they came in and made their way to the living room. I watched them squirm in this foreign environment, and I made no move to hide any of it. They talked to me for a few minutes then quickly exited, leaving me some tracts that I would never read. I am sorry that I exposed them to that, but none of those things seemed abnormal to me at the time. I did recognize that what they observed would seem abnormal to them, but I could not see that my view of the world was tainted by the calluses I had built up to sin. I recognize now that calluses had blurred my vision and contributed to my pursuit of joy in the artificial and counterfeit things of this world.

The calluses in my life had been wearing off over the months at Overcomers and what was left was new skin, sensitive to the things of this world. In Steinbeck's novel, *Of Mice and Men*, Curly wears a Vaseline-filled glove on one hand to keep that hand soft for his wife. He chooses to protect his hand from calluses so that it was left sensitive and pleasing for his wife to hold. Walking with Jesus doesn't require a Vaseline-filled anything. As Jesus cleans you inside and out, He takes out the old and replaces it with something new.

> *Therefore, if anyone cleanses himself from what is dishonorable, he will be a vessel for honorable use, set apart as holy, useful to the master of the house, ready for every good work. So flee youthful passions and pursue righteousness, faith, love, and peace, along with those who call on the Lord from a pure heart.*
> —2 Timothy 2:21–22

Over the months my heart had softened, and I was seeing the harshness of the world for the first time. I understood that the armor of God was not some poetic mumbo jumbo; it was a necessary thing to protect that softened soul. It also is circular in its reasoning. The more you put on the armor, the more you are protected. The more you are protected, the softer your skin becomes, and the more you need armor. Ephesians 6 is a focus we should all have if we want to have any chance of defending ourselves. We should put on the belt of truth, the breastplate of righteousness, shoes of the gospel of peace, the shield of faith, and the sword of the spirit each day before our knees get off the cold bedroom floor.

Recently, I was working on a project where I was shoveling a couple of cubic yards of topsoil out of the bed of a truck and alongside a road. There was a time in my life when I could shovel all day long without barely breaking a sweat. Ten minutes into this project I had giant fluid-filled blisters at the base of each thumb. I had not put on gloves or realized how the shovel would wear on my now "callous-less" hands.

The f-bomb moment at the free clinic was a similar experience, or it could have been. The worst thing that could have happened would have been for me to not recognize that I was exposed and allow a callous to build back up. Over the years I have not noticed those callouses building up more times than I would like to admit. A few weeks ago, my pastor talked about how we justify what we watch on TV. He said, for example, we lay judgment on those that watch X, but we watch Y because it only has one nude scene and the Lord's name is only taken in vain three times. Man, am I guilty of that justification. This type of thinking causes a callous, which is not from God, to be built up on our hearts.

The good news is that callouses are not permanent unless we let them be. We get an opportunity to reset, put back on the whole armor of God, and watch Jesus melt those soul-hardened spots right back off. Whenever I get off course, I often think of that day in the waiting room of the dental clinic and know that there is hope. The more I cling to Him, the more my life reflects the sweetness and softness of Jesus.

A few years ago, Bill's sweet wife Janine passed away after a long fight with cancer. At her memorial I heard one of the most impactful stories from one of her friends and a longtime volunteer for Miracle Hill, Peg Hudson.

Peg recounted that she had a conversation with Janine about the day she would get to heaven. Typically, people will say that when they get to heaven, they want the Lord to say, "Well done my good and faithful servant, enter into your reward." Janine had a different take on it. She said that when she gets to heaven and is face to face with Christ, she wants Him to look at her and say, "You look like Me."

In each one of us, underneath all the callouses of the world, is Christ. The more we rest in Him and keep our armor on, the more of Him is revealed. Like a good sculptor, He removes all the extra stuff to reveal what is beneath. For those of us who trust in Jesus, He is underneath.

In the stories of Mary and Martha we can learn several lessons. In Luke 10 Mary rested at the Master's feet instead of doing chores. Her sister Martha was busy working, which is noble, but not the same as resting and reclining with God. In another instance in the twelfth chapter of the Gospel of John, Mary is judged for wasting oil as she extravagantly puts the oil on Jesus's feet and wipes them with her hair. As Mary walked out of the house that day, she didn't necessarily look like Jesus physically, but have you ever thought about the fact that she smelled like Him?

Like Janine, I want to look like Jesus. I want to recline in His presence daily. I want the callouses of the world wiped away and for everyone who comes in contact with me to smell the aroma of Christ.

Chapter 13

FIRST DRINK, ACT II

If any of you lacks wisdom, let him ask God, who gives generously to all without reproach, and it will be given him. But let him ask in faith, with no doubting, for the one who doubts is like a wave of the sea that is driven and tossed by the wind. For that person must not suppose that he will receive anything from the Lord; he is a double-minded man, unstable in all his ways.

—James 1:5–8

I wish I had spent more time reading and studying James when I was in the program. We, who believe, know that the Lord's word doesn't come back void, but I recognize now that I could not see the true depth of my depravity then, nor could I understand how much I still yearned for the world to accept me. James's words fell on deaf ears if I had read them at all.

After completing the program, I was ready to get back to the world, and I did what every person does. I chose which parts of the Bible I was going to follow, and I chose which areas I consciously or subconsciously still believed that I knew better than God. Certainly, we do not think about it that way when we are in the moment, but humans tend to forget about the Lord's omnipotence, omnipresence, and omniscience.

I graduated in November of 2003 and by all accounts, I was in the best mental, emotional, physical, and spiritual state I had ever been in my life. I spent a few months helping the staff in a Servant Leadership program, but eventually my time at the mission came to an end, and I had to start returning to the world.

As the Lord does, He was gracious to me on my exit. Because of two men's commitment to the Lord and Miracle Hill, I was blessed with a job working for a couple of great Christian men, Mark and Ricky. Mark went so far as to allow me to rent a trailer to live in, instantly solving my housing issue. I got plugged into my first church and continued a relationship with one of the counselors who was mentoring me and teaching me how to be a lay counselor. By all accounts, life was great.

The problem was, I was only at eighty percent. I was willing to do most, but not all, that the Lord wanted me to do. I was also willing to do most, but not all, that recovery required of me. It wasn't that I was choosing to do terrible things by the world's standards. On the contrary, I was only compromising on the things that I viewed as not mattering a great deal. I listened to music that I had been warned to stay away from. I watched movies with questionable content, but I was still working daily on walking with Jesus and trying to conform my life to a world that was new to me. I eventually found a friend group that was all young college-aged Christians. They drank a little, but they weren't addicts, and so who was I to say anything to them? I felt like I was starting to "fit in" and wanted desperately not to stand out in the crowd. Instead of hiding in the gutters, I was attempting to hide in plain sight. It turns out that some of those compromises mattered a great deal.

Most addicts believe that everyone knows they are in recovery as if they are wearing a visible clown nose everywhere they go. Maybe a better analogy is the idea of the scarlet letter. In Hawthorne's book, the scarlet letter is attached by society to identify the adulterer. In recovery, we are often the ones attaching the letter to ourselves—a big fat **A** for addict.

As we struggle with figuring out our identity, we want to hide that **A**, thinking that the world's judgment is upon us for the sins of our past. We falsely believe that we stick out in a crowd and work to make sure that we don't look different than anyone else. This false narrative about who we are, naturally creates compromise unless our identity in Christ is firm and our resolve is strong. I was in a state of compromise and frankly did not see it. We do this when we measure ourselves against what we believe the world wants from us rather than what God plainly shares that He demands of us.

James shows us the result of these compromises:

> *Blessed is the man who remains steadfast under trial, for when he has stood the test he will receive the crown of life, which God has promised to those who love him. Let no one say when he is tempted, "I am being tempted by God," for God cannot be tempted with evil, and he himself tempts no one. But each person is tempted when he is lured and enticed by his own desire. Then desire when it has conceived gives birth to sin, and sin when it is fully grown brings forth death.*
> —James 1:12–15

When he is lured and enticed by his own desire. Wow. James hits us with this truth about the origin of our desire and sin. The devil didn't make me do it. There is no conspiracy to make me do wrong. It is me.

I can't blame anyone else for the decisions I made during this time. While on one hand I was walking in step with Jesus, I still so desperately wanted to please man that I believed that my compromises were in line with His people. They often were, but I should have been working to be in step with Him rather than them because guess what, they were all broken sinners too. Most wanted acceptance the same way I did. Fitting in was quickly killing me and at first, I couldn't see it. Temptation for me had become the idolization of normalcy.

Over the years I have warned thousands of our guests of this reality. Most people come into recovery because they want to learn how to beat their addiction rather than submit to God. They want to learn how to cope rather than humbly admit defeat. The best truth that we can learn as humans is that we can't, and God can. If we, for one minute, believe that victory comes from us, then we are fated to be a character in a tragedy in the long run.

> *The heart is deceitful above all things, and desperately wicked; who can know it?*
> —Jeremiah 17:9 NKJV

My heart was still sick. I was no longer burdened by the crimes and failures of my past, but my identity wasn't rooted and grounded in complete pursuit of Christ. Dare I say that all these years later, after another lifetime of brokenness and pain, I can still see areas that I am measuring myself by something other than the reality of Christ and the truth of Scripture. However, through the admission of my own brokenness and recognition of those places by wise counselors and friends I have in my life, I can see where I am falling short. But during this season, I had not fully grasped the freedom of transparency or the necessity of accountability. I was still hiding the parts of me that I thought were undesirable to others. I lasted about a year with an eighty-percent commitment.

> *But be doers of the word, and not hearers only, deceiving yourselves. For if anyone is a hearer of the word and not a doer, he is like a man who looks intently at his natural face in a mirror. For he looks at himself and goes away and at once forgets what he was like. But the one who looks into the perfect law, the law of liberty, and perseveres, being no*

hearer who forgets but a doer who acts, he will be blessed in his doing.

—James 1:22–25

Eventually, I drank. I can give you a series of events that led to my first drink on the right side of sobriety, but none of them matter. The lesson is that I made one compromise after another until I forgot the pain of my past and *"as a dog returneth to his vomit, so a fool returneth to his folly"* (Proverbs 26:11 KJV). I was a fool.

When I play the tape all the way back to the earliest compromise, I can see it had nothing to do with blatant sin returning to my life. It was about valuing and prioritizing things out of order. One of the disciplines I learned at Miracle Hill was having a daily quiet time that started with reading my daily proverb. Even when I moved into my own place, I maintained that daily proverb and prayer seven days a week, fifty-two weeks a year.

One day, I woke up late for work and skipped my devotion time. The next day I resumed and thought nothing of it. A few weeks later, I skipped a day again. Then it was two days a week. Then without realizing it, I stopped doing it all together, and I didn't even see that it was gone. It was so gradual that I became accustomed to not doing my daily proverb, and as a result, I had unintentionally cut myself off from my power source.

It was some months after the daily proverb was gone before I took my first drink. I wasn't isolated and alone when the decision to drink came; I was sitting at a dinner table at a restaurant with other young believers. I had been the only person with a glass of water at dinner many times, and my overwhelming desire to fit in made my justification easy. I reasoned that I was a "drug addict," but not a "drunk." I believed that I was far enough away from my brokenness that it was "OK." I thought I would fit in better if I looked like everyone else, instead of caring that I look like Jesus.

That first night the worst thing that could happen to someone who just threw away their sobriety happened: Nothing happened. I had a drink, I went home, I went to bed, and got up the next day, and nothing was wrong. In that moment I believed my own lie; I wasn't an addict, and I could handle it.

Although I justified my decision, shame came back quickly, and this fueled my desire to use. The peace I had earned through devotion and trust in Jesus was gone within days. The way I saw it, I had disappointed everyone in my life when I made a conscious decision to drink. I was scared to look those I loved in the eye. By this point my brothers had tentatively come back into my life, and their caution and skepticism were proven warranted by my actions. What do we do when we are afraid to face ourselves? We do our best to hide and lie. I stopped answering calls, again. I lied about the truth, again. Isn't our capacity to forget who we are amazing?

It didn't take long for alcohol to take me as deep and dark as all the drugs in the world ever could. Once this barrier was crossed, it was easy for me to cross other barriers with ease. One domino led to another, and I was off to the races.

Chapter 14

WIDE IS THE ROAD

Enter by the narrow gate; for wide is the gate and broad is the way that leads to destruction, and there are many who go in by it. Because narrow is the gate and difficult is the way which leads to life, and there are few who find it.
                                        —Matthew 7:13–14 NKJV

The decline in my life after that first drink was slow at first and then swiftly picked up speed. One minute I was employed, housed, in community, part of a church, and in healthy relationships, and the next minute I was broke, busted, and disgusted. I again found myself experiencing life with a giant God-shaped void in it—the difference being that I had tasted what was good in relation to Jesus.

As my employment ended, I made the decision to move, again, and start over, again. I walked away from the stability I had built in my life and moved to the middle of the state with a friend. He and I made more compromises; I hid some recreational drug use from him, and eventually, he and I began drinking together. We wound up at the bars and clubs together. Then he quickly began separating himself from the looming train wreck that was my existence, and I went to the bars and clubs alone. Then I didn't go anywhere. I began drinking alone. Doing drugs alone. Doing everything alone. I gave you a picture of this season at the beginning of the book. Did you notice that there was no mention of the Lord in it? As the compromises piled on top of each other, He got pushed further and further out of the picture and out of my mind. Moments of sobriety would bring Him to the forefront of my mind only to be drowned back out. The armor came off, and the callouses grew. I had quite literally forgotten the face of my Father.

My favorite verse in Proverbs says, *"A man who isolates himself seeks his own desire; He rages against all wise judgment"* (Proverbs 18:1 NKJV).

This is what we do in our sin. We isolate, and our sickness goes deeper. I have ministered to thousands of people who struggle with addiction and in one way or another, we all seem to do this. We isolate physically or mentally or both, retreating into the darkness of our own minds.

I do not believe I completely lost sight of the presence of God in my life during this time, but I worked diligently to hide His voice in each box of wine.

I bounced around to a few jobs but couldn't stay employed. My brothers, who were talking to me again, began to suspect that something was off in my disjointed communications with them. My only friend and roommate essentially disappeared from the house we shared. Eventually, I resigned myself to my life of addiction and knew the end was close.

I do not mean "the end" in some melodramatic way. Suicide again seemed completely reasonable to me. When you believe you have nowhere left to turn and when the shame overwhelms you, then the idea of not having to fight anymore can seem romantic—the ultimate solution.

My tendency to chemically solve my problems again went from casual use, to recreational, to daily until it became the blood that coursed through my veins. I have had many conversations over the years that start with the question, "Why couldn't you just stop?" And I think it is hard to explain. Along my journey someone explained it to me like this: "Take a deep breath and hold it. Hold it as long as you can. Hold it until it hurts. Now take a breath. That desire to breathe is like the pull of addiction. That first breath is like using itself."

It is as if there is no other alternative, and you not only can't think of another choice, but in that moment, there is no other choice. I am not excusing the choice but explaining that it seems like the only one. Clearly it isn't, but in a confused stupor, rationality is not often present.

Anyone who has ever had the unfortunate experience to drink or use drugs with me will tell you that I was a pass-out drunk. I used so fast that my body would eventually shut down and force me to sleep or pass out. I do not understand the physical reason why my body reacted this way, but I believe it is a defense mechanism. If my conscious mind will not stop me from poisoning myself to death, then my unconscious mind steps in and makes the decision for me. I learned this about myself and would typically take either of two courses of action. Either I would drink knowing I would pass out with the intention to pass out and melt away from the world, or I would work to prevent passing out with the result being a blackout.

A blackout is when you "miss" large amounts of time and can't recall what you did though you clearly did something. There were times when I would start drinking or using, and I would "come to" a day later, somewhere completely different, not knowing how I could have gotten there. This period of relapse contains some of the worst blackout experiences of my life, and I do not know how I survived without deeper scars.

On one occasion, my roommate and I went to the bars in downtown Columbia, South Carolina, near the USC campus. About two hours before we left for the bars, we started to pre-game, or drink before we left to meet people. I could drink a lot in two hours.

Eventually, we left home, and, for the record, I was already drunk. Unfortunately, I was also driving. On the way, I knew I wasn't long from the world of sleep, so I stopped and purchased some Yellow Jackets, powerful stimulants sold over the counter in most gas stations under various names. Within an hour of getting to the bars, I was separated from my friend, and after that, my memory gets hazy at best. I remember buying some weed and ecstasy from some guy in a bathroom. None of these things should be mixed with alcohol, the combination being potentially fatal depending on the amount.

Sometime later, I woke up in a cul-de-sac. I was extremely confused and had no clue where I was, so I began driving again. Around four thirty in the morning, I came to behind the wheel as I was driving down a road in the middle of nowhere. This means that for the past four hours, I had been mobile, but I had no memory to account for the time. I drove for fifteen minutes before I found a gas station and stopped for alcohol and directions. Turns out, I was in Camden, South Carolina, thirty-five miles from the bars where I started. There is no reason I am still walking the face of the planet other than the grace of God.

Over the course of a couple of years, I had alienated all the healthy relationships I had cultivated. I threw away all the goodness God had inserted in my life. I ran through all my remaining resources. I disappointed everyone who cared about me. Not only had I done all these things, but I had done them **again**, and I wished for death.

I don't know what was different the day I decided to fight back. I had called one of my remaining friends, Erika, and she had allowed me to come over to her house. I believe I spent a few days there while contemplating my choices, which I reasoned to be just three:

1. Die.
2. Pretend that I could control my life.
3. Ask for help.

I sat in her living room petting her little dog and going back and forth on my choices. If I choose death then I don't have to fight anymore, but the closer I got to that option, the more I knew that I wanted to live. Remember, I knew God, and I knew that He wanted something different from me and for me. Much like the analogy of addiction, desiring life is like gasping for breath as well. When my life was void of "life," I was suffocating. In the recesses of my mind, I remembered experiencing life in Christ, and I wanted that back.

I did not believe the lie that I could control my life. I was in the midst of my own destruction, so the self-inflicted wounds were real to me at the time, and I couldn't blame them on my past.

Last, I could ask for help. There was so much fear in this that I felt frozen. Arguably more than on the first round. I was ashamed of my actions. I was fearful of the consequences. I didn't want to have to climb out of the hole I was in.

God gave me strength, and I picked up the phone and I called Curtis Pitts. As soon as he answered, which he did quickly, I started to cry. Hearing his voice was like hearing Jesus speaking to me in real time. He told me to calm down. He asked where I was. He asked me how quickly I could get back. There was no judgment. There was no anger. There was only love.

> *For judgment is without mercy to one who has shown no mercy.* **Mercy triumphs over judgment.**
> —James 2:13 (emphasis added)

Chapter 15

OVERCOMERS, ACT II

oming back to Miracle Hill was a lesson in humility in many ways. The day I was checked in was a Sunday and when I got there, all the other guys were at church; I had the dorm to myself. I set up my bed and locker in Overcomer fashion and lined my shoes under my bed. I put on what I perceived as my hippest outfit and went outside to read a book.

Directly outside the dorm was a little cement pad with benches on it. I sat down with my back to the sun and began reading. Eventually, the guys returned, and we had lunch. After lunch, men typically do one of three things on a Sunday. Either they take a nap, as it is the only time during the week when that is possible, or they go outside to play volleyball or they gather for some other social activity. This was winter, but we are in South Carolina, so it was mild, and the men went out to play volleyball. I went back to my bench. Over the course of a few hours, a few men tried to interact with me, but I was so full of shame that I gave clipped responses and avoided their eyes.

I pretended to be reading, but what I was really doing was thinking about all the people that I had "let down" and all of the people that I would be forced to interact with in the coming days. I thought of Ed and Frances Phillips, Miracle Hill's longest running volunteers and the leaders of the Overcomer Choir. I thought of the counselors. I thought of Curtis Pitts and Bill Slocum, and the disappointment they obviously and certainly felt about my life.

Eventually, it was time to go in for dinner, so I got up from the bench. I went inside and walked by the mirror. It took me a minute to realize something was off. I went back to the mirror and to my horror, I saw that one side of my face was completely sunburned from sitting in the same spot for six hours that day. With my dress and my attitude, I wanted to be unapproachable and super cool. In reality I was scared, and I was a fraud. I walked to dinner truly two-faced and a divided man for the world to see.

The next morning, we started our week, and I learned that Mark Alverson had his office in the dorm. I nervously paced around the dorm that morning dreading the moment when he got in, terrified to face what I had done to my life.

He showed up, and one of the guys said, "Mark, Ryan Duerk is back."

I could hear Mark from where I was in the dorm and heard his exclamation, "Really?! Where is he?"

I gathered my courage and walked around the corner. In that moment he realized I wasn't there to visit; I was there because I needed help. Mark took one look at me and opened his arms. I walked into them and sobbed. There was no condemnation in his embrace. There was no judgment. There was only love.

Over the next few weeks, I saw everyone again. The staff members and volunteers were tender with me. They expressed excitement to see me but also grieved with me over what I viewed as loss. There was no condemnation. There was no judgment. There was only love.

The second round of Overcomers was exponentially more difficult than the first. On the first round I was a sponge soaking up truth in every imaginable way. I had not known anything about recovery or Jesus or how to live. By the time I graduated in 2003, I knew more than most about recovery, and I was a son of the Most High, heading out into the world with a sharpened sword.

Round two, in 2007, I already knew much of what they had to teach, but I had not applied it. I knew recovery and could teach a college-level course on it, but I had not walked in it for long. I had experienced freedom from hundreds of hours of counseling concerning the wounds from my life, yet I had disregarded those lessons and chosen the easy path.

I knew the truth of Scripture but had chosen not to bathe in it daily.

I knew where the path of addiction led but had gone down it anyway.

I didn't need an education from Overcomers, I had to look deeper within my soul and determine why I kept going back to the empty wells in my life.

Pretty quickly I came to the eighty percent realization about round 1 and knew what the first step on this journey had to be.

And as he was setting out on his journey, a man ran up and knelt before him and asked him, "Good Teacher, what must I do to inherit eternal life?" And Jesus said to him, "Why do you call me good? No one is good except God alone. You know the commandments: 'Do not murder, Do not commit adultery, Do not steal, Do not bear false witness, Do not defraud, Honor your father and mother.'" And he said to him, "Teacher, all these I have kept from my youth." And Jesus, looking at him, loved him, and said to him, "You lack one thing: go, sell all that you have and give to the poor, and you will have treasure in heaven; and come, follow me." Disheartened by the saying, he went away sorrowful, for he had great possessions.

—Mark 10:17–22

This passage describing Jesus's interaction with the rich young ruler has often been used for sermons about the love of money, but the message Jesus gives to him is much deeper than greed. Jesus tells him to sell everything and follow Him. The Jesus I know doesn't tell lies or exaggerate, so I am left to believe that Jesus meant what He said. Jesus wanted all of the man; not eighty percent of his faithfulness. The passage says the man was grieved because he wasn't willing to give up his comfort, dare I say his disguise. Jesus wanted him to see that everything he is and has is worthless outside of a relationship with Him. The man chose the world over following Jesus, and I had been doing the same thing. Jesus doesn't want eighty percent of our lives. He wants it all. He demands it all. He knows that we will fall short, but that doesn't diminish His desire for us to wholly walk with Him.

The first step in my recovery was to give Jesus 100 percent control of my life. I could no longer live with a mask on or show people who I wanted them to see. I needed to live with my identity in Christ on display for the world. There could be no more compromises, and I had to equip defenses so that if they showed up, there would be guardrails in place to help me to see them. I recognized quickly that the only way that Ryan's life would work, is if Ryan wasn't driving the bus. Jesus had to have complete control. This, much like salvation, is a singular decision that we make over and over each day.

The second step of the process had to do with identity. When I walked out of Overcomers in 2003, I was a Christian, who was an addict in recovery, who was a chameleon trying to fit into the new world. I needed to be so rooted in my identity in Christ that this is all that I was. I couldn't care about the things of the world. I had to get to a place where it wouldn't matter what the world or the enemy said about me; I would know who I was.

There are two cultures in every recovery program. There is the culture set by the program and its administrators, and there is a culture set by the clients. Often these two cultures are very different from each other, and each group works to protect the autonomy of its own culture. Make no mistake, Overcomers is filled with broken addicted sinners, most of whom are master manipulators with a criminal history as we have already discussed.

I grasped onto the identity truth and the 100 percent commitment truth with all that I had in my being. I did this honestly but also out of fear and necessity, knowing that I had no other choice. As a result, I began to stand out in the crowd everywhere I was. I am sure that I looked no different to the staff than others because they know that the guests work to make the staff see what they want them to see. With my Overcomer brothers, however, my commitment was not well received. In my immaturity I saw everything as black or white and had no concept of the graceful gray in life. Everything either became lawful or not. My friend group shrank, and I only spent time with those I perceived as being serious about doing something different.

There are usually a few guests in our facilities who have this same devotion to their new life, and the other guests typically make life difficult for them. It is not that I thought I was holier than others, but rather I was fearful of what life would be if I gave even an inch to the enemy. I had been down that road, and that was a road that led to death.

Now there is in Jerusalem by the Sheep Gate a pool, in Aramaic called Bethesda, which has five roofed colonnades. In these lay a multitude of invalids—blind, lame, and paralyzed. One man was there who had been an invalid for thirty-eight years. When Jesus saw him lying there and knew that he had already been there a long time, he said to him, "Do you want to be healed?" The sick man answered him, "Sir, I have no one to put me into the pool when the water is stirred up, and while I am going another steps down before me." Jesus said to him, "Get up, take up your bed, and walk." And at once the man was healed, and he took up his bed and walked.

Now that day was the Sabbath. So the Jews said to the man who had been healed, "It is the Sabbath, and it is not lawful for you to take up your bed." But he answered them, "The man who healed me, that man said to me, 'Take up your bed, and walk.'" They asked him, "Who is the man who said to you, 'Take up your bed and walk'?" Now the man who had been healed did not know who it was, for Jesus had withdrawn, as there was a crowd in the place. Afterward Jesus found him in the temple and said to him, "See, you are well! Sin no more, that nothing worse may happen to you."
—John 5:2–14

John 5 is my favorite story in the Bible to talk about addiction.

The pool is a real place, and people went there believing that when the water was occasionally stirred by an invisible creature, the first person in would receive healing. They went there every day waiting for a miracle and begging for scraps much like the modern-day person standing on a street corner.

Right off the bat, you can see one of the dilemmas in the story. Let's say that the pool is real; then what is the problem if you are blind? How about if you are paralyzed? Even if the pool was real, there was no way for those people to receive the healing that the pool offers.

This is misplaced faith; we do it all the time. We think that if we accomplish some goal, everything will be OK. If we can get into the right relationship, save enough money, get a better job, have cool friends, or only drink on the weekends, then everything will be OK. But none of those things can heal us. The adjectives used in the story are *blind, lame,* and *paralyzed*; I was all these things.

The Greek word for blind can refer to either physical or mental blindness—blind to the realities of the world or, in my case, blind to the Lord's truth and reality. Lame means deprived of a foot, limping, not working as it should. Paralyzed means dry and withered, such as a dry land; it's the idea of something being frozen, and in that I think of fear.

I was blind to the truths of the world, lame to live within its rules, and fearful of man.

The man in John 5 had been that way for thirty-eight years. I had been stuck for a decade and a half. A person can stay stuck in a sin or a way of life when they misplace their faith and place their bets on a lame duck.

When Jesus finds the man, he asks him a very specific question: *"Do you want to be healed?"* The idea in the question is not whether he wants to be relieved of the effects of his disability, but rather, does he want complete change? Fill in the blank with me:

- I once was lost, but now I am _____.
- I once was paralyzed, but now I am _____.
- I was blind, but now I _____.

The man answers Jesus in the same way that we often answer Him when He asks us the same question. We make an excuse as to why we can't find healing in whatever it is we are putting our faith in. Jesus then gives him a command: Get up, pick up your mat, and walk.

Everything in the man's life would have told him that what this man, Jesus, was suggesting was impossible. Imagine for yourself what your body would look like after being an invalid for thirty-eight years. I think of every picture I have seen of the people in Auschwitz. All his muscles would have atrophied, and his identity would have been rooted in the truth that he could not, under any circumstances, get up.

People often misquote Scripture to say God helps those who help themselves. While the Scripture never uses that phrase, the essence of the idea is found in Jesus's command. Jesus is essentially saying to the man: "If you want your life to be forever changed, then I will give you all the strength you need to change it, but you have to do it. **You** get up. **You** pick up your mat. And **you** walk away." The man believed him. He got up, picked up his mat, and he walked away. How powerful.

There are two important things to note about the mat. First, it was illegal to move the mat on the sabbath, but Jesus was more concerned with grace than man's law in this instance. Second, the mat was about identity. Jesus didn't want the man to forget that he was changed. He didn't want the man to start looking for his bed and remember it was back at this empty well of misplaced faith. Jesus wanted the man to know that his identity was no longer in his brokenness but rather in his healing.

In verse 14 Jesus finds the man and tells him to sin no more that nothing worse may happen to him. We have no reason to believe that the man was an invalid because of sin, but Jesus doesn't want his life to become clouded by sin and run the risk of forgetting who he is.

I was this man. I had walked away from the pool and had forgotten that I was healed. I was following Jesus, but instead of listening to His voice beckon me to follow Him, I let the noise of the world overwhelm me. I eventually walked straight back to the pool, with my mat, and sat down. I forgot who I was. All of us who know Jesus run the risk of this happening in our lives. The only difference between me and you are the misplaced faiths we trust in, the type of sin that blinds us and binds us, and the identity we believe in when we are sitting by our own pool.

I finished Overcomers a second time in the fall of 2007 with a commitment to the Lord—to follow Him, no matter what. I was taking it a day at a time, as we learn in recovery, but each day I was working to be 100 percent submitted to what He had for my life. I never wanted to find myself back on that mat by the pool begging for scraps.

Recently, Miracle Hill's chief development officer, Jacob Edmisten, shared a verse the Lord had used in his own quiet time.

I wait for the LORD, my soul waits, and in His word I hope; my soul waits for the Lord more than watchmen for the morning, more than watchmen for the morning.
—Psalm 130:5–6

Jacob shared with me and others his deepest desire to yearn after the Lord like the watchmen in the night. As I think of this Scripture, I think also of Psalm 42. I believe I was learning that the enemy might surround me but that if I seek the Lord and hope in Him alone, then all will be well. I wanted then and now to yearn after the Lord. I encourage you to consider this as you encounter the soothing balm of His word.

As a deer pants for flowing streams, so pants my soul for
you, O God.
My soul thirsts for God, for the living God.
When shall I come and appear before God?
My tears have been my food day and night,
while they say to me all the day long,
  "Where is your God?"
These things I remember, as I pour out my soul:
how I would go with the throng and lead them in procession
to the house of God
with glad shouts and songs of praise, a multitude keeping
festival.
Why are you cast down, O my soul, and why are you in
turmoil within me?
Hope in God; for I shall again praise him, my salvation and
my God.
My soul is cast down within me; therefore I remember you
from the land of Jordan and of Hermon, from Mount Mizar.
Deep calls to deep at the roar of your waterfalls;
all your breakers and your waves have gone over me.
By day the LORD *commands his steadfast love, and at night*
his song is with me,
  a prayer to the God of my life.
I say to God, my rock:
  "Why have you forgotten me?

Why do I go mourning because of the oppression of the enemy?"
As with a deadly wound in my bones, my adversaries taunt me,
while they say to me all the day long, "Where is your God?"
Why are you cast down, O my soul, and why are you in turmoil within me?
Hope in God; for I shall again praise him,
*   my salvation and my God.*

—Psalm 42

Chapter 16

NOT FOR ME

After I had been an intern with Miracle Hill for a few months, I began to get anxious about what would be next after this season was over. As is typical for individuals in this situation, I had no real resources, very few transferable skills, and a lot of debt—relationally, financially, and in every way imaginable. Each day I felt the tick of the clock as I got one day older and one day closer to departing the nest. As such, I knew I needed to get a job, and I really wanted to work for Miracle Hill. I don't believe I had enough spiritual discernment to say that I was called to work with the homeless, addicted, and lost, but I certainly felt safe, secure, and filled with purpose in my role at the mission.

Over the preceding months I had narrowed my possible career choices to three options: house renovator, recovery counselor, or funeral home worker. My thinking for the first two options was that I enjoyed construction and knew recovery. The third option was due to an experience I had at the funeral home when my mother died. When my oldest brother Chris and I went to the funeral home to finalize things, the man who sat with us was exactly who and what we needed him to be during the experience. He was clearly a natural empath and skilled counselor. When we first arrived, Chris and I were dealing with the situation with laughter, and he reflected that. When it was time to view Mom's body, Chris and I got serious, and he sensed that and changed this mood to match ours. He had a lasting impact on me for his honest reflection of our feelings and his ability to be patient and kind. I had also spent several years working as a meat cutter and had seen my fair share of blood, and I wasn't squeamish. Combine those skills and you get a funeral home worker. At the time, my reasoning and logic seemed correct to me and thus funeral home worker became one of my leading choices.

For several months I asked the Lord to show me what He wanted me to do. I prayed every day for His guidance and wisdom and eventually, two of those ideas started to sound silly, and one sounded correct. This was as close to throwing a fleece out as I had done in my spiritual walk, and God honored my faithfulness by giving me clarity through peace. He quieted my spirit around the idea of sticking around Miracle Hill.

Additionally, I had a fear about leaving the structure and community that had contributed to my health. I rationalized this into the idea that I was meant for ministry, especially ministry as Miracle Hill. Honestly, my pursuit of working for Miracle Hill was probably sixty percent fear, which is not a great basis for a career decision.

Making decisions based on fear had been a leading thought process that contributed to the destruction I caused in my addicted life, and I was struggling to shake off that thought process. Another way to say how I felt would be to say that I was terrified to come out from underneath the safety net that existed at the mission. Jumping back into society with both feet seemed foolish to me and after experiencing real peace, I was unwilling to risk losing all that I had gained. I simply did not trust myself to make wise decisions and believed that if I stayed where I was, I would be OK. We try to steer our guests away from this kind of thinking.

The truth of the Bible teaches us that if God takes you somewhere, He will give you everything you need to keep you there.

> *Be strong and courageous. Do not fear or be in dread of them, for it is the LORD your God who goes with you. He will not leave you or forsake you.*
>
> —Deuteronomy 31:6

Compounding this issue for me was pride. I thought that because I was such a good worker, I should be given a counselor's job along with all the benefits and respect that went with that title. It shouldn't matter that I was spiritually immature and inexperienced in counseling, that I only had a GED, and that I had a criminal record.

Eventually, I was brought into the director's office and told that they wanted me to pursue a ministry job. Excitement flooded my entire being at the prospect of moving from a guest relationship to that of a peer with the men who had fought so gallantly for my soul. Here was my chance to financially provide for myself and gain a respectable career. Then, I was told what the job was: I was asked to apply to be a worker at our food warehouse.

I was heartbroken. I didn't want to do that unglamorous job. Didn't they know that I was capable of so much more? Didn't they recognize how much potential I had and that this job was beneath me?

> *When pride comes, then comes disgrace, but with the humble is wisdom.*
>
> —Proverbs 11:2

I said that I would pray about it, knowing this was the approved Christian verbiage when confronted with a choice that you do not want to accept. My emotions instantly made the decision to leave Miracle Hill and go back to flipping houses or managing an automotive shop, or any job that fit my perceived level of greatness. But Jesus and sobriety had given me enough clarity to know that I should not make a quick decision. I had learned enough to know I needed to go two or three rounds with God first.

Do not be anxious about anything, but in everything by prayer and supplication with thanksgiving let your requests be made known to God. And the peace of God, which surpasses all understanding, will guard your hearts and your minds in Christ Jesus.
—Philippians 4:6–7

I spent the next couple of days with nothing else on my mind except what do to about this opportunity. Luckily, I was still close enough to my addiction that I knew I didn't want to jeopardize my sobriety. In my prayer life over those days, I experienced God as silent. I couldn't get out of my head long enough to let God speak clearly to me through His word or His people. I talked to every "wise" person I knew on the planet and was frustrated that they would not tell me what to do. They wanted me to make the decision. I finally landed on one piece of truth.

Every time I try to map out my life, I destroy it, and every time I let others guide my life, God blesses it. I knew what would happen if Ryan did what Ryan wanted to do. I would be successful for a few months and then. . .

The years under the wisdom and discipleship of the amazing men and women of God at Miracle Hill life had been great. Making very little money as an intern, I had lacked for nothing. Working endlessly each week, I felt rested. People were beginning to trust me. I was healthier than I had ever been. I was more emotionally, physically, and spiritually stable than I had ever been in my life. It was undeniable that my life was immeasurably better than I could have ever hoped or imagined because I wasn't driving it into a ditch.

I decided to trust those who had come before me, in a life-altering decision, for the first time in my adult life. I walked into the director's office against what my flesh was screaming at me and asked for an application.

Similar leaps of faith permeate most of the major decisions in my life since meeting Jesus. I learned from this first major crossroad that if I trusted God with my life, He would come through. The outcome is not always what I imagine, but his faithfulness in it is unquestionable.

I would love to be able to say that after that time, I never questioned God or His people again, but that wouldn't be true. On occasion God's emissaries have suggested that I do something I am uncomfortable with—take a job, shift a position, or try a new thing. I, like many of us, am extraordinarily hardheaded. When faced with a major decision, my flesh first goes to doubt and then skepticism. I lean on fear and question. I counselor shop, meaning I go from one person to the next trying to find someone who agrees with my logic rather than whatever perceived poison I am being asked to ingest. However, God is patient and kind; He meets me every time at that point of fear and says:

Come to me, all who labor and are heavy laden, and I will give you rest. Take my yoke upon you, and learn from me, for I am gentle and lowly in heart, and you will find rest for your souls. For my yoke is easy, and my burden is light.
—Matthew 11:28–30

In the beauty and reassurance of that Scripture, let it not be lost on any of us that God has a yoke and a burden. A yoke goes around your neck to move you in various directions, and a burden is weight on your back. The Lord's yoke is easy, but it is still a yoke. His burden is light, but it is still a burden. Not everything that the Lord asks you or me to do seems like the best answer, and it may not be easy as He is stretching our endurance and patience in His desire for us to look more like Jesus. But God. He always gives us what we need to make it to the next destination on the journey He has us on.

I am learning through my walk that the road He is leading me down is not free of potholes. There aren't rainbows and unicorns behind every bend of the road. Certainly, decisions get easier every time I choose to trust Him rather than myself, but one of the keys to my life is having copious wise counselors surrounding me in everything I do. When I poll the right audience, I seem to hear God speaking more clearly to me. I also experience a fair amount of freedom in that I am not alone in my decisions. Yes, as a human I was born alone, and I will die alone, but God's grace provides a lot of amazing people to help us while living in that singular dash on our tombstones. Furthermore, each time I recognize that God is the driver, and I am the passenger, I realize that I have never, nor will ever, be alone again.

Chapter 17

FIRST DAY

On my first day at the food warehouse as an official employee of Miracle Hill, the Lord immediately went to work helping me to redefine both myself and my false ideas about ministry service. I walked in to meet Tom Callahan, my new boss and mentor; I was both nervous and excited for what life might bring through this adventure. I had no clue that God had prepared Tom with a specific set of skills that He would use to shape me. Ultimately, Tom played an important role in my growth. His term of endearment for me was instantly created as he said, "Grasshopper, come over here so we can fellowship for a spell." He then informed me that we were waiting for some special guests, "two important dignitaries," to meet with us before we started our day.

Shortly, Jim Wolff and Bill Slocum walked in the door. At this point I think you should all know who Bill is and what he means to me. He was, and still is, an amazing mentor, friend, and spiritual father in the faith. Jim was the Thrift Ministries warehouse supervisor, but I didn't know him well. What I knew was that he was a longtime trusted employee, beloved by all of Thrift and the guests who worked in Thrift, and he was a lifelong friend and accountability partner to Reid Lehman. Although I did not know Reid, I knew enough to understand that he was a key leader in the ministry. Today, Jim is recently retired from the ministry, but I know I could call him tomorrow to get a heap of wisdom in a pinch.

Back then my gut reaction was to be fearful. What had I done? Why were these men coming to see me on my first day on the job? After Bill and Jim arrived, we sat down at the table in the back of the warehouse and these three men began to talk to me about ministry. They unpacked their thoughts about ministry and hammered the fact that this was not just a job. This was not just a way to earn a paycheck and cut my teeth, but it was my first real opportunity to be Jesus to the world around me while being blessed to earn a living while doing it. Essentially, this was my welcome to vocational ministry speech.

Yet the experience was so much more than that; I remember Bill talking about the weight of ministry while Tom hammered in the idea that whatever I would be doing, he was no longer my boss; Jesus was. Jim reminded me the Scripture is clear that greater responsibility in the Kingdom brings greater expectation and requires greater accountability.

Whatever you do, work heartily, as for the Lord and not for men, knowing that from the Lord you will receive the inheritance as your reward. You are serving the Lord Christ.
—Colossians 3:23–24

What does it mean to serve the Lord? As a believer it is easy to contextualize service to Jesus when we are doing something on a church mission trip or serving in the preschool on Sunday morning, but what does this mean in the environment of the rest of our lives?

I concede that working in a vocational ministry setting makes the Colossians concept easier to grasp as Jesus is in our culture and speech, but I assure you that everyone in a vocational ministry setting struggles to keep the Lord in the boss's chair.

These men were trying to convey to me that my life, our lives, are truly not our own. Throughout our day, we might be the only believer that someone encounters, and whether we view it as fair or not, those people are going to judge Jesus based on who we are. Furthermore, the God of the universe, who knows all and sees all, is the author of our potential to impact this world for His glory. When we commit our lives to Christ, our lives are a resource at the King's disposal.

After a lengthy discussion around the table with these mighty men, they asked me to put my chair in the middle of the floor of the warehouse. Beside boxes of baked beans and crates of cereal, they surrounded me, laid their God-serving hands on me, and prayed a prayer of commission over me into the ministry. I was so deeply moved and humbled.

For the weeks leading up to that day, I had viewed the opportunity in the food warehouse as something I had to do to get to the next thing. In a moment, the Lord worked through these amazing men to show me that this job was something I was getting to do for Him.

How different would our lives be if every opportunity to do anything, especially the things we don't want to do, was viewed as an opportunity to do something for and with the Lord? As I began to move about the warehouse in the dust and the grime, I started to see the true potential and gift of serving Jesus with my life. I no longer saw it as a compartmentalized life divided into what was His and what was mine, but all of it, poured out as a drink offering like Christ did for me. What an honor we have to be able to call Jesus friend, Savior, and boss.

As the weeks went by, I began to see the work of the employees in a new light. Across the breadth of the ministry, I saw these faithful men and women who were giving daily of themselves for little to no personal gain. They drive trucks, pack boxes, make meals, clean toilets, fix lights, talk with the destitute, pray with strangers, work on computers, count widgets, hang clothes, and advocate for those who can't advocate for themselves. They love children and speak the truth of God's word when given opportunity. They pour themselves out each day because Jesus told them to.

In *God Wears His Own Watch,*[1] written by Miracle Hill's longtime CEO, Reid Lehman, Reid talks about the matriarchs and patriarchs of the ministry who decades ago worked without pay, selflessly giving to the Lord.

Well, their spirit is alive and well in the staff of Miracle Hill today. What the Lord has built here is an army of nearly three hundred warriors for the faith. They do a thousand different tasks each day, but for the exact same reason as their predecessors: Jesus.

I pray that each of us understands this truth about our walk with the Lord—that we are getting to engage in His story as we go about our daily lives, regardless of what we do for a living. I pray that each of you understands that as well. While Miracle Hill is vocational ministry by definition, each of you, who trusts Jesus as Lord and Savior, work in vocational ministry according to the Bible. Each of us, whether a butcher, baker, or candlestick maker, has the same calling of Christ to serve man as we serve the Lord. What a challenge and what an opportunity.

---

1 Reid Lehman, *God Wears His Own Watch* (Spartanburg, SC: Miracle Hill Ministries, 2010).

Chapter 18

MANNA

Working for Tom Callahan at the food warehouse proved to be one of the greatest tools the Lord used to shape my life. Tom was disorganized, gregarious, and loud—all of which grated against my broody, introverted OCD tendencies. Each day we would start with devotion when the helpers from the Overcomers arrived. I would make it a point to get there several hours before anybody, so I could clean up the warehouse and actually deserve a break before we took one. Tom was so intentional to stop what he was doing to talk and minister to anyone who walked into the warehouse. He would leave whatever task he was doing to engage in relationship. This meant that over the years, thousands of tasks had been left perpetually undone, and when I started working there, the warehouse was in a state of disastrous chaos. This turned out to be a good thing for me, in that I love a challenge and organization, and the warehouse provided me with an outlet that I did not view as focused on internal heart change. I had been working on a program for so long that doing something physical and breaking a sweat was a beautiful change for me.

Initially, Tom fought me a little on my thoughts on organization, but he eventually realized that I have a gift for organization, and he got out of my way. We developed a rhythm where I would work to correct a mess, and he would continue to accidentally create one. I was younger and faster than he was though, and I started to make progress, and the warehouse gradually started to take shape around me. I remember the day when I could finally drive the forklift into an aisle and turn it around without hitting anything or anyone. It was glorious.

Tom continually complicated my pristine warehouse whenever we had shoppers come in throughout the week. This ministry rescued food from across the Upstate and then redistributed it to the various shelters, programs, foster families, and other ministries. We would stop what we were doing to help these individuals get what they needed when they came to the warehouse. Having this as our main function gave me my first taste of what it meant to be God's people outside the Rescue Mission. We also gave out twenty food boxes a day to disadvantaged families, and creating those boxes was part of the daily routine.

One behavior that Tom did constantly drove me crazy; he would run into the warehouse and start shouting, "Let's gather together and pray! The people need X," X being whatever product that he thought was in demand and hadn't been donated lately. The products we prayed for would be anything from green beans to ground beef, from syrup to salad mix, and everything in between. Tom wouldn't just say a quick prayer for these things. He would stop everyone from working and gather us in a circle to fervently pray for "the thing" for what seemed like hours. In reality it was probably only about fifteen minutes. If you happened to walk into the warehouse during this time, you would get sucked into Tom's prayer vortex and couldn't leave until he was satisfied that we had sufficiently sought the face of God. He sought God for everything.

And whatever you ask in prayer, you will receive, if you have faith.
—Matthew 21:22

Tom had faith in excess. My life experience and personality were not accustomed to this faith-focused behavior, and I struggled with it daily. I would sit in his circle thinking of all the things that I needed to do and complain to myself about what a waste of time this was. I just did not get it.

One day Tom came rushing into the warehouse during an especially busy time of the day and yelled for us to gather because the people "needed" juice and jelly. Inside my head I wanted to scream at him that we were busy and didn't have time for this nonsense, but I was obedient (again part of my recovery) and begrudgingly gathered with everyone else in the middle of the warehouse for Tom's prayer.

Tom went into a typically pleading prayer for God to bring the people juice and jelly. In retrospect he typically followed an ACTS (Adoration, Confession, Thanksgiving, Supplication) model of prayer and would talk to the Lord about how good He was, then confess our shortcomings, then thank Him for His goodness, and then ask for the Lord's intervention in whatever need we had. In these moments he would call upon the name of the Lord to deliver His people from the oppression of not having proper nutrition. He asked for God's forgiveness as he talked to his Lord and Savior. He cried literally and figuratively for God to help. His devotion to prayer was coupled with a deep commitment to modeling faithfulness to all around him. He wanted to be Jesus and talk to Jesus about everything.

I sat there with a bad attitude and waited to get back to work. Eventually, the prayer time was over, and I got back to doing what I perceived as important that day. We organized, loaded, cleaned, and prepped boxes. We sweated and did our hourly push-ups. We grunted and strained and cleaned potatoes. We unloaded trucks and loaded boxes in the back of people's cars.

About an hour later I heard the unmistakable sound of airbrakes. I went outside to find a semitruck parked beside our rollup door and a driver climbing out of the cab. This was an unscheduled delivery, so I went to see what the driver needed. I arrived at the truck about the time the driver was cutting the banded lock on the fifty-two-foot trailer and opening the rear door.

Inside the truck was pallet after pallet after pallet of juice and jelly. I was floored.

Never had I experienced the power of prayer and the power of God in such a tangible way. My eyes were opened to the reality of God in a completely new way, and I was humbled to the depths of my soul. For the first time in my walk, I saw a prayer answered specifically and immediately. Because God is God, He didn't just drop off a bottle of juice and a jar of jelly, He dropped off a whole tractor trailer load. I truly didn't know what to say to anyone as the reality of the God I served settled into my heart.

It seems that a peach farmer had donated the rest of the goods from that year's crop, so we had peach jam, peach jelly, peach cider, peach preserves, peach butter, and every other peach product imaginable. There was so much peach product that it eventually became the manna of all Miracle Hill facilities. The guests became so tired of peach that they began boycotting the juice and jelly within a few months.

> *Do not be anxious about anything, but in everything by prayer and supplication with thanksgiving let your requests be made known to God. And the peace of God, which surpasses all understanding, will guard your hearts and your minds in Christ Jesus.*
> —Philippians 4:6–7

After that experience I began seeing God provide in a whole new light. A few months after the juice and jelly, we received a call from a frozen food company to come and get some pallets of frozen beef and macaroni. When we arrived at the cold warehouse, we learned that there were dozens of pallets with thousands of meals on each. Tens of thousands of pounds of beef and macaroni. Initially, the new main course was a big hit in the facilities and was nicknamed Chili Mac. The kitchens doctored the meal in every way imaginable. There was Chili Mac and Cheese, Chili Mac with Peppers, Chili Mac on a hamburger bun, and every other combination you can imagine. After a few more months, everyone was sick of the meal and worked even harder to use it to be done with it. Eventually, we got to the last pallet and the people rejoiced across the land. Within a day of finishing the Chili Mac, a truck brought us around ten pallets that were a thousand pounds of ground emu each. I didn't even know that ground emu was a thing; again, God had provided. There were Emu Burgers, Emu Spaghetti, Emu Tacos, and Emu Manwiches. I do not believe that we specifically prayed for Chili Mac or ground emu, but the Lord knew what we needed and provided it in His time.

After seeing God provide in such real ways, I felt strengthened in my own prayer life. I began praying in true belief that I was connected to the ultimate power source, and as a result, I saw God daily moving in my life in new and, at times, jarring ways.

Occasionally, we would get an amazing donation, but not in an amount that could be distributed to all the facilities. Often, I would pray about who the Lord had in mind for the specific blessing. One day we received a 50-pound box of shrimp. It clearly wasn't enough for everyone, so I set to prayer and clearly felt the Lord lead me to keep it back for the ladies from Renewal who were due to shop the warehouse that afternoon. When the ladies showed up that day, I told them I had a surprise for them in the freezer. We walked back to the freezer and piled into its freezing depths. I dug through the pallet in front of me and produced the huge box of shrimp to which the ladies immediately began weeping. Apparently, right before they left the center, they had gathered to pray specifically for seafood. The Lord's timing is perfect. If we work to listen, He allows us to be a part of His grace.

I had been so wrong in my reactions to Tom's priorities, and I learned so much from him. He taught me to pray with faith, believing that God would answer. God worked during this time to teach me that He is listening. Tom taught me that relationship is more important than task, while God taught me to love others who don't look and think like I do. Tom taught me to believe God's word while God taught me that His word is alive.

Eventually, Tom trusted me enough to let me take our huge box truck out to pick up rescued food across the Upstate. I had the opportunity to meet amazing men and women working for different companies that just wanted to help and would hand over thousands of pounds of goods to the ministry. Sometimes, they wanted a tax receipt but more often than not, they didn't. They may not have worked in a ministry setting, but they were working for the King. Tom would get to work in the morning and yell, "Grasshopper (his nickname for me), go get in JJ; the Lord is giving us green beans this morning!" Off I would go to whatever address he handed me. After a few months of this, I finally asked why he called the truck JJ. Can you guess? It stood for Jehovah Jirah; the Lord shall provide.

Over the year that I worked with Tom, I saw that precious name of God come to life. As Reid Lehman shares in *God Wears His Own Watch*, the history of Miracle Hill has been continually defined by such George Mueller moments. Let me tell you that God is still showing up and showing out at Miracle Hill. He provides, in His time, every time.

Looking back, God truly became Jehovah Jireh for me on that juice and jelly morning at the food warehouse so many years ago. It is easy to forget that we have ready access to the most powerful being in creation. God wants us to share our needs and life with Him. He wants to show up and show out in our lives. The same God who provided manna to the Israelites thousands of years ago is waiting for us to talk to Him right now. How amazing and humbling.

Occasionally, I get the opportunity to talk to our guests about prayer. When I do, I ask them if they want to know if God answers prayer. Obviously, they want to know as do we all. The punchline is that there is only one way to find out if He answers prayer: we must pray.

If we pray and seek the face of God, I promise that He will answer. He may not always give you what you want, but that doesn't mean He isn't responding. "No" and "Not now" are acceptable answers from Him as well.

> *And this is the confidence that we have toward him, that if we ask anything according to his will he hears us. And if we know that he hears us in whatever we ask, we know that we have the requests that we have asked of him.*
> —1 John 5:14–15

If we seek and knock and share our needs with Him, he has an opportunity to respond. If we don't, then we do not get to look back and see His goodness at work in our lives. I urge you to trust Him and talk to Him; He is still in the juice and jelly game.

Chapter 19

SIMBA AND PUMA

I had the opportunity to move into Miracle Hill's new transitional housing community, Grace Point, when I exited Overcomers the second time. Several years earlier Miracle Hill was blessed to find themselves in possession of some property in Greenville that had two old farmhouses on it. The ministry began developing the property into its first transitional housing subdivision. Quickly, two more houses were brought onto the property. When I moved in, only three houses were active, and construction was underway to add a road, drainage, and infrastructure to the community. For the first few months, we had to park up on the main road and walk down to our house precariously balancing on wood planks to avoid the mud.

I was more than willing to do this, as for the first time in many years, I had a home that felt like it was mine. I was surrounded by men who were on a similar journey to my own, and I was content. We ate dinner together, had house meetings, and talked about Scripture. On the weekends we went to meetings together, or the movies, or other social activities that we planned, but we did them sober for the first time in most of our adult lives.

Within a few months, some men would relapse and much like a warzone, we would grieve their exit then keep moving forward. The occupants of the beds would change, but the mission never faltered, and some of us found a home at Grace Point Transitional Community.

We were not allowed to have pets, but one evening a couple of stray dogs showed up while we were outside grilling. One was a khaki-colored pit bull mix we named Simba, and the other was a black lab mix we named Puma. While we couldn't have pets, we secretly began feeding these dogs, and they quickly became part of the pack, or we became part of theirs. How fitting that two homeless dogs found the community filled with homeless addicts.

Months went by, and we would occasionally see Puma and Simba around the neighborhood. Eventually, we earned their trust, and they would let us pet them at will; leftover steak seems to have that effect on dogs.

One day Simba showed up by himself. It was late fall or early winter, and we couldn't figure out where his partner in crime was. Eventually, someone saw him going into an open door that led to one of the house's crawl spaces. We decided to follow him to see what he was after, and in the dim light of the crawl space, we could barely see Puma tucked into the back. One man crawled in after him and quickly recognized that the dog was hurt, growling, and scared.

We banded together and decided to get him out even if we got bitten in the process. Over a long and sweaty hour, we fished him out, and could see clearly that he had been shot twice at close range by a pistol. The neighborhood where we were located was not the best. As soon as we got him out, he ran away. We spent the next week trying to find him so that we could get him help but couldn't find him anywhere. We even called the pound hoping they could catch him, but they too came up with nothing.

About a month later, we finally caught him one winter's day and decided we would clean the wounds. My buddy, Matt, and I turned on the hose and got some antibacterial soap. We did our best to move his fur and clean out the bloody matted mess it had become. To our horror we observed maggots on the wound; we lost control of the dog and watched him run into the dark woods. To add insult to injury, now he was not only shot, but wet and covered in soap. We didn't see him again for a long time.

In early spring we scheduled a cookout for the whole community and got to work grilling burgers and steaks for approximately twenty men. By then the community was flourishing with a road, six houses, and lots of activity.

In the middle of the cookout, we looked up toward the hill and saw about seven dogs emerging from the woods and headed toward us. This pack of dogs was as diverse as we were, small dogs and large dogs of various breeds and mixes. At the front of the pack was Puma. All the fur was missing from his upper back and entire left side, but in its absence, you could see the first signs of a new coat growing in its place. I believe he had licked all the fur off in an attempt to clean the wounds. Puma, having never been to a veterinarian, had walked off two gunshot wounds.

Looking back on the experience I see all of us so clearly reflected in the dog's experience. When we are hurt, we growl and bite those who are closest to us. When we perceive death on the horizon, we isolate and try to go it alone. When we are healthy, we see the safety and benefit of being part of the pack.

The clarity we all need is to see that the pack is there to help us when we are hurting the most and when we think we are dying. I can see so much of my own response to pain and trauma in Puma. I bit so many people who loved me dearly. I isolated so often when there were people who loved me and wanted to hold me in the midst of my storm.

Bear one another's burdens and, so fulfill the law of Christ.
—Galatians 6:2

The hard part is that letting someone bear our burdens requires vulnerability on our part. Sure, it's easy when we are shot and lying in a hospital bed, but it's so much harder when the pain, trauma, failure, or broken parts of our lives are not easy to see. In recovery there is a saying that we are as sick as our secrets. I see this so often in the shelters, recovery centers, and church meetings I attend.

Miracle Hill uses a Christian adaptation of the Twelve Steps of recovery. The Twelve Steps often get a bad rap in Christian circles, but Jesus was at the center of the original program; it was later changed to make the Twelve Steps more palatable to people of different faiths or no faith at all. All we do is put him back in his rightful place, at the center. I believe that each step is biblical. Let me summarize them for you and you can be the judge:

1. I am no good.
2. God is good.
3. I will put Him in charge.
4. I need to look deep within myself and see what's good and what's bad.
5. I need to confess those things to someone else and God.
6. I need to be ready for the Lord to clean house.
7. Now that I am ready, I will ask Him to do that.
8. I need to know everyone I have wronged and be prepared to make it right with them.
9. Now that I know who, I need to go to them personally, if possible and healthy for everyone, and own my junk.
10. I need to keep the closet clean and be vulnerable and transparent always.
11. Through prayer and meditation, I need to keep God first every day.
12. I should tell others about Jesus and help them when I can.

Sounds biblical, huh? There is a strong argument that every Bible-believing, Jesus-loving, God-fearing Christ follower needs those Twelve

Steps in their life. Often people in recovery argue over what is the most important step. I think the argument is pointless as each step carries its own weight in a person's life; they certainly have in mine.

I believe that the fifth step can make or break someone's recovery because of secrets. The step says that we, *"Admitted to God, to ourselves, and to another human being the exact nature of our wrongs."* This is the natural follow-up to the fourth step, which requires a person to look deep within themselves and uncover all the skeletons and broken places in their past; it is where we get really honest with ourselves.

Unfortunately, people will often do a fearless inventory of their life but only share ninety percent of that with another person out of fear. They have this amazing opportunity to have someone share their burden, but their secret is so heavy and their shame so thick that they are unwilling to unpack it with someone else.

By the time I had gotten to the inventory step in my journey, I was either so sick of being sick, or so committed to the process that I left no stone unturned in the written inventory. Eventually, the day came when it was time for the confession and in those days, we did it in a group setting.

I remember walking into my counselor Eddie's office where we were having group with my paper in hand. While I was filled with a profound amount of fear, I also felt ready to stop carrying this burden alone. I don't remember walking through the inventory itself, but I remember not leaving anything off. I shared my deepest darkest secrets, wounds, crimes, traumas, and sins with that group of men. I told them things I had never uttered to another human being before. They all gathered around me and prayed for some time that God would heal the broken places in my life.

I remember leaving the room and walking back through the Overcomer dorm and out into the yard. I made it past our volleyball court and around a corner where I didn't think anyone could see me before my knees buckled and I dropped to the dirt weeping uncontrollably for some unknown length of time. Eventually, the tears dried up, and I could stand. For the first time in my memory to that point, I stood with my back straight, a thousand pounds lighter. My secrets were not just mine anymore.

Therefore, confess your sins to one another and pray for one another, that you may be healed. The prayer of a righteous person has great power as it is working.
—James 5:16

Puma hid from the world in the crawl space under a house, with bullet wounds, hoping that his wounds would go away. While I believe that he licked most of the fur off his side, I do not think that he could have reached his own back. Whoever had wounded him had shot him straight through his back and out his side. The only way that those entry wounds got clean is if he let the pack lick his wounds for him.

Clearly, he did.

He must have become so weak that his growling and biting ceased, and he was ready to let the pack in close enough to help. He was so beaten down that even if he tried to isolate, the dogs who loved him tracked him down and helped.

I am Puma, and so are many of you. We need to take great care to see the shattered places in our lives and let the pack in. Jesus is the greatest burden bearer of them all, and there is no hiding from Him. He, however, knows how desperately we need each other, and He built the Church as a model for us. None of us were meant to carry the loads of life alone.

After sharing my past, I had hundreds of hours of counseling to help me deal with those broken places, but it all started with confession and my acknowledgment that God did not intend for me to live a life isolated and alone.

Chapter 20

INTENTIONAL

During my time at the food warehouse, we had a specific schedule. Around eight every morning a line of people formed outside the front door of the food warehouse. At ten, we opened the door, and the first twenty families in line entered to receive food boxes. Those who were in need could come once a month. The people who came for food boxes were as varied as the guests in our facilities—old and young, educated and not. What they all had in common was that, for one reason or another, they needed help and financially were not able to make ends meet.

The contents of food boxes varied from day to day. We typically filled one banana box with nonperishable items such as canned vegetables, pasta, or casserole mixes, and we filled the other box with perishable items. Sometimes, the perishables included some type of vegetable I had never heard of such as bok choy. Does anyone know what to do with bok choy? Additionally, we would give each family frozen meat and a couple of loaves of bread. What we gave rested entirely on what had been donated.

When each family came in, another staff member named David Waldrop or I greeted them, took some information from them, and then escorted them to one of the cubicles behind us where one of our prayer volunteers was waiting. The prayer counselor's job is simple; all they have to do is ask if they could pray for the person. Sometimes, family members say no, and the prayer counselor then escorts them to their food and returns to their cubicle to pray for them silently. Sometimes, the family takes the opportunity to share their struggles and lets the prayer counselor pray for their needs. Occasionally, the prayer counselor may discern a deeper struggle and have an opportunity to share the gospel.

Our prayer counselors are amazing men and women of God who faithfully give of themselves just to spiritually engage with another human being. They also come from a variety of walks of life, and the Lord has used each of their stories to bring them into service at the food warehouse.

One day I was working at the intake booth when an older gentleman came in for the last box of the day. He looked to be in his mid-eighties and was not happy to be there. He sat across from me as I took his information, and it was clear that he would have rather been anywhere but giving his personal information to some punk kid. I quickly finished my part of the process and ushered him into the cubicle behind me to meet an amazing man of God and longtime volunteer named Dave Holland.

Now the cubicles along the hallway are not far apart from each other and have no doors on the front for safety purposes. Therefore, the hallway is loud during food box time, and I could often hear everything that was happening in the cubicles behind me.

As this man moved into the cubicle with Dave, I couldn't help but to overhear their conversation. Dave started the conversation by asking the man how he was doing and if there was anything he could pray about for him or his family.

The man retorted that he didn't need or have time for the prayer. He was in a hurry and needed to be on his way.

I do not know what Dave heard in the man's voice, but apparently the Holy Spirit shared with Dave that this meeting was a divine appointment. Dave asked if he could share a story with the man and produced an Evangecube from the desk.

An Evangecube is a portable evangelism device often used by missionaries to present the gospel when there is a language barrier. (If you want to know more, Google *Evangecube*.) What this man didn't know was that Dave had been traveling to Barranquilla, Columbia, a few times a year and was a spiritual ninja with the Evangecube.

I clearly remember what the man said to Dave as he produced the Cube: "Son, I have been in church since I was a little boy; I don't need you to tell me about Jesus."

Dave made the decision to ignore the man's rebuke and kindly shared the simple truth of the gospel.

1. Separation of man from God due to sin.
2. Christ's death on the cross.
3. The tomb.
4. Christ's resurrection.
5. His sacrifice to make a path back for us to relationship with God.
6. Two outcomes from two choices: heaven or hell.
7. What it means to be a follower of Christ.

The room was silent for a few minutes after Dave finished his presentation. The man had heard the beauty and simplicity of the gospel and understood what it meant to choose Jesus. After a time, I heard the man speak again through his own tears. He said, "Son, I have been in church for over seventy years, and I have never heard that before." The man immediately prayed to receive Jesus as his Lord and Savior.

Dave, and so many others like him, make a decision to show up and be available to the Lord. In this case Dave was evangelically minded, and so the volunteer task he was doing fit directly into his passions and skills. Many other people just show up and offer to do whatever is needed around the ministry.

And I heard the voice of the Lord saying, "Whom shall I send, and who will go for us?" Then I said, "Here I am! Send me." And he said, "Go . . ."
—Isaiah 6:8

Each year at Miracle Hill, thousands of people make that choice. They show up and do whatever is needed. They scrub toilets, pray, cook meals, teach classes, clean vans, and spread mulch. In recent years, the hours they contribute are the equivalent of dozens of additional full-time staff members. Sometimes, all that results from their work is a clean toilet and an honored God, but sometimes God has a divine appointment awaiting a humble servant.

Whatever skill you have, I promise that there is a use for that skill. All the Lord needs any of us to do is say, *"Here I am Lord, Send me."*

Several years ago, we had the opportunity to fold another food ministry into ours which quadrupled our warehouse space and ability to rescue food. This merger created Miracle Hill—From God to You.

We still do the food boxes, and now in addition to the amazing prayer warriors who show up to pray with the guests, we also have a full-time case manager who tries to help people stabilize their finances and life if they need assistance. People are still meeting Jesus.

I do not know what was going on in Dave's life the day he met that man in the food warehouse. I am sure he was busy as we all are, but he prioritized serving over comfort. He chose to show up and gave God the avenue to show out. I also have no idea what happened to the elderly man with whom Dave prayed that day. Perhaps he left and went back to his own misery; then again, perhaps he didn't. Either way, as much as I can know on this side of heaven, I trust he met Jesus that day. He heard the truth of the gospel, and his life was forever changed as a result.

If you live near a ministry or helping organization and you are passionate about their mission, please consider serving. God is after your time, talents, and treasures and can use any of those things or all three. The most important thing you can do to support these ministries is to pray for them, but if you are willing, and not too chicken to try something new, consider showing up and getting your hands dirty. You will not regret it.

Chapter 21

FEAR

When I left home in my teens, I entered this endless cycle of alcohol and drugs, sleeping on couches, time in jail, many different jobs, and a lot of lies. As I went through life, I would inevitably run into people that I knew from my youth. They would ask what I was doing, and I would tell them all the same thing:

I am working at so and so, and I am getting ready to go to college. I took my SAT when I was in high school and did pretty well. When I took the test the first time, I scored 1080 after I had studied hard for the test. I decided to take it again and didn't study at all; instead, I went out partying the night before and actually did better that time, scoring 1160. I have been avoiding college as I try to figure out what to do, but it's time, and I am starting in the fall.

The truth is I never even took the SAT in high school. I do not remember why, but in my spiral, I somehow neglected the test. I had no intention of going back to school because my life was out of control, and I had zero direction.

Naturally, I had come up with this intentional and elaborate lie to hide who I really was. I bet I told that lie a hundred times to anyone who asked about my trajectory in life. I told that lie so many times to so many people that I started to believe it myself. Each conversation forced the lie to embed deeper into my soul, and I had a response prepared for whatever detail I was asked about.

The only contact I had with college was when some friends who were attending a local university let me crash on their dorm couch for a few months. Eventually, I was arrested on campus while committing some crimes and taken to county jail. Therefore, the only official document that had ever connected me to a college told me that I could never legally step foot on that campus again. That might be the definitional opposite of going to college.

Once I went to work in the ministry, I knew that I needed to go to college to progress further in life and in my hopes for ministry. In this desire, I was forced to face for the first time in my adult life the truth of my lie. I wanted to go to college, but I didn't have the faintest idea how I was supposed to do that. No one had ever shown me, and I was in such a fog in high school that I had not paid attention to the details. I didn't know about applications or funding or schedules or majors or anything that someone needs to know to pursue a higher education. Stoned for most of high school, while my friends were scheduling tours of colleges, I was playing "hey mister" at the corner store. This is where my friend Joey Hines enters the story.

While I was in Overcomers, I met a guy who was my age but experientially had a completely different life than I did. He had a great homelife growing up and had earned a college degree; now, he had a wife, his own business, and overall success in life. He was my age but was a board member of Miracle Hill and came in weekly to teach a class at Overcomers. We couldn't have been more different from each other.

Joey and I didn't become friends right away because that wouldn't have been appropriate. He was in a position of authority, and I was a guest of the ministry, but we did have a connection in common; his wife and I went to high school together.

After I went to work for the ministry, Joey and I met regularly for breakfast to talk through issues. I was rebuilding my life, and he had life experience. He chose to take time out of his busy life to spend it with me. He does this for other men to this day. I knew right away that Joey was someone I could trust—someone who wanted something better for my life.

At one breakfast meeting, I confessed to Joey that I needed to open a bank account but believed that no bank would consider me because of all the banks I defrauded in the past with overdrafts and bad checks. I was vulnerable with him, sharing information that was embarrassing and potentially criminal. He told me at the end of the breakfast that he had an idea but to give him a few days.

Several days later, he got in touch with me and told me he was picking me up and taking me to see a friend of his. We jumped in his truck and drove to a regionally run bank where he introduced me to his friend, Susan. Joey then looked at me and said, "Tell her your story and tell her your problem."

Joey had quickly become someone I trusted, but he was asking me to bare my soul to a stranger. I imagined that I would finish talking and the police would come in the door to escort me away. I don't remember the details of the conversation, but I did what he told me to do. Amazingly, Susan agreed to open a secure savings account in my name.

Today, I know Susan well as she was my banker for over a decade. Back then she had no reason to open that account. She and I had only one thing in common, Joey.

Eventually, the secured savings account became a secured checking account, and eventually a regular checking account. Ultimately, I fixed my banking and credit issues completely, but it all started with a stranger taking a risk on behalf of someone she knew, and I would guess a healthy dose of Jesus.

Today, Joey is one of my best friends. He is still active at Miracle Hill as a volunteer, but that has nothing to do with our relationship. He is someone I trust unquestionably and someone I love deeply. We have learned over the years that we aren't different at all; each of us is a broken sinner in need of a savior.

What he taught me that day was that some of our problems are not ours to carry alone. We cannot fix them by ourselves. The only sure way to never fix a problem is to never address it, yet by sharing my fear and being vulnerable, the problem started to magically dissolve. This is not always the case, but the fact is, we can't address an issue that we can't define and do not have experience managing. Admitting ignorance is often what God is asking us to step into.

Back to the college dilemma. I knew that I needed to go to college, but I was filled with fear. Going to college was like climbing Mount Everest to me. However, Joey had taught me what to do. I drove down to Greenville Technical College one afternoon after work and sat in the parking lot for a few minutes before going in. I was still scared, but Joey and the Lord had empowered me to handle the situation.

I walked into the lobby and went up to the information desk. There was a sweet older woman sitting at the desk, and I shared with her an intimate and vulnerable truth from my life. In an instant, exposing myself to a stranger, I said: "I want to go to college, but I don't know how."

This woman became my personal angel that day as she stood up and said, "Follow me." She took me to a computer and said, "Fill out this application and when you are done, come back and see me. If you have any questions, I will be at that desk."

Over the next few hours, she walked me from application to financial aid to registration to advising. I don't believe that was part of her job. She picked up my life where Joey and Susan had set it down. By the end of the day, I had a schedule and was set for my first day of class.

It turns out that getting into college was pretty easy. The fear of taking this step had been built up in my mind for so many years. It was filled with a decade of lies that I had told others, but more importantly, that I had told myself. We often build things up in our head, repeating lies of the enemy to ourselves until they overrule the truth.

> *Death and life are in the power of the tongue, and those who love it will eat its fruits.*
> —Proverbs 18:21

This verse is usually considered from the perspective of how we talk to others. For many of us, our tongue holds death because it is the release valve for the lies, we tell ourselves. The tongue returns false narrative to our ears and ultimately our soul, draining us. We spew out more lies to defend the weaknesses we see in ourselves. These secrets are usually not based in truth or reality, but as your only critic, you will never know the difference. How much shame do we carry that isn't even real?

Recovery teaches us to vomit out truth to each other. It tells us that we need to be completely open and vulnerable to another human being, trusting them with our secrets. If we choose to do this, then the person we share with gets to share the weight of those secrets. More importantly, this exercise helps us to face our own reality and share it with God. He isn't surprised by our truth because He knows it anyway, but the exercise releases us in a way that is indescribable. This fearless transparency also works to unify our disjointed identity.

In addiction I was a kaleidoscope of different people depending on who I was talking to and what I was trying to accomplish; I was a shape-shifter. To find peace, all those personas need to be destroyed until the true identity emerges, void of false narratives and lies. For believers, our identity in Christ should reign at the center.

The less we hide from each other, the less we hide from Jesus. He is able to reconcile these discrepancies about who we are so that we can look deep within ourselves and be OK showing that person to the world. Christ washes away our sins and makes us whole again as we are reminded in the old gospel hymn by Robert Lowry and William Doane:

What can wash away my sin?
Nothing but the blood of Jesus;
What can make me whole again?
Nothing but the blood of Jesus.

Oh! Precious is the flow
That makes me white as snow;
No other fount I know,
Nothing but the blood of Jesus.

If we find the strength to engage, God will provide each of us with a Joey or a Susan or a little old lady at a desk to help us navigate the world and share the weight of our fears. More importantly, Jesus bore the weight of our sin on the cross. Who are we to carry it again?

Being washed by the blood doesn't mean that we will be perfect. It means that it doesn't matter that we are not. His perfection is the driving force in our lives, not our own attempt at perfection. His truth and identity matter much more than our own and do not falter under the weight of the world, rejection, or people. His identity covers everything.

I have heard many times that we should never pray for patience because if we do, God will put us in situations where we are faced with impatience. This is true but not because God wants us to feel bad about ourselves, but because He wants us to let go and let Him be in charge. He doesn't struggle with impatience. Praise God for that.

In ironworks, the forge is used to purify precious metals by introducing extreme heat into the cleansing process. Impure metals are placed into the cauldron, heat is added, and everything gets melted down. The blacksmith then scoops out the impurities that rise to the surface. This process is repeated over and over again. The blacksmith knows that the precious metal has become pure when enough impurities are removed that he or she can see their reflection in the molten metal.

Jesus does the same thing to us. We invite Him in and ask Him to remove some impurity from our life. Facing our baggage and lies about who we are brings extreme heat and pressure, and then if we let Him, God removes the impurity. The longer we allow this, the more the Son can see Himself in us. This is sanctification.

Praise God for the heat and pressure. Praise God for the understanding of my own faults and failures. Praise the Lord that He brings people into our lives to help navigate when we are scared others might see the impurities and run. Praise God that he doesn't want to leave me the way I am, have been, or will be. He wants to see Himself in me.

> *How much more will the blood of Christ, who through the eternal Spirit offered himself without blemish to God, purify our conscience from dead works to serve the living God.*
> —Hebrews 9:14

Chapter 22

SAFETY IN AN ABUNDANCE

A nother principle that is often repeated in recovery programs has to do with romantic relationships:

Get a plant in the first year of sobriety. If it is still alive when you get to year two, get a dog. If the dog is still alive at year three, then you are ready to date.

The reasoning behind this principle is that the plant and the dog show whether you have grown to a place where you are not self-focused and are prepared to consider the thoughts and feelings of another creature, eventually working your way toward relations with a human being. At Overcomers this gets boiled down to one simple rule to live by: No dating for a year.

As someone who was laser-focused, I found it easy to comply with this rule. That is not to say that I didn't struggle with lust and loneliness, but I just removed the thought of dating from my mind. Busyness kept me from struggling a lot during that first year.

A year doesn't seem that long in the face of years of brokenness, but remember that when someone completes a long-term program, they are the healthiest that they have been in forever. They look and feel better and are tired of being alone. Seeking a relationship too soon has been the downfall of many a person in early recovery. It is not that the person is a bad person, or that the person they are engaged in a relationship with is a bad person, it simply has to do with priorities. God calls us to prioritize Him first, then others, then ourselves. If we don't have practice doing this, then it is easy to get it out of sync and reap the results of that decision.

If you ask most people in recovery whether they want to date someone who is healthy, they will say yes. Defining it further as someone who is healthy mentally, emotionally, physically, and spiritually they will still agree.

News flash to the person in recovery, that person does not want to date you. They wouldn't be healthy if they did. This is a hard truth. A person who is healthy throughout their life wants someone else who is healthy in all areas. In early recovery, we do not fit that definition. So, if you find yourself easily dating someone a week after you get out of a homeless shelter, run away.

Regardless of my commitment and understanding of the dilemma, I struggled with my eyes and hormones. I was a healthy man, and God gave us all a libido, which He intended for the marriage bed. But between the ministry, college, church, and outside activities, I didn't have a tremendous amount of time to think about it, and I didn't feel alone. For sure my thoughts and actions were not always pure, but I ran from relationships.

In some of my downtime, I would often go downtown and sit at one of the coffee shops reading, writing, and people watching. As women my age walked by, I would daydream about what it would be like to know them, date them, or love them. More importantly I dreamed about what it would be like to be loved by them for who I was growing into. That being said, my foundation was granite, and I would not budge from the dating principle.

The year commitment came and went, and I was still focused on my recovery and new life. During this season I had transitioned from the food warehouse to being a junior counselor for Overcomers at the Greenville Rescue Mission. I was living in transitional housing, going to school, and working on a Christian Counseling credential. On top of those pursuits, I was learning how to help other men like me.

Every morning, I would drive into downtown Greenville and stop at a local coffee shop to get a coffee before heading to the rescue mission. Often when I was there, Curtis and I would run into each other before work, as he was getting his morning tea.

Most mornings there was a sweet girl there, working at the register and making the coffee. Over time we formed a friendship of familiarity. This evolved to where neither Curtis nor I had to tell her our order anymore. We would exchange pleasantries; I would get my coffee and be on my way.

One day I walked into Curtis's office, and he asked me why I wasn't dating. I told him that I was committed to the year of no dating and was focused on what I was doing. He mentioned that I was several months past the year. I shifted the subject and went back to work.

A few weeks later Curtis brought it up again in our morning meeting. I repeated the same answer, and he sat back and thought. Eventually, he said, "What about the girl in the coffee shop? She seems like a nice girl."

I laughed it off, and he retorted, "If I see you in the coffee shop again and you haven't asked that girl out to dinner, I am going to embarrass you." I went back to work thinking that Curtis was joking. He was not.

As you can imagine, the day came when I was getting my morning coffee and in comes Curtis with a big grin on his face.

"Well, good morning, Mr. Duerk."

He got behind me in line, and I could feel the pressure of his presence; I was desperately trying to get out the door before he had an opportunity to talk.

My coffee done, I grabbed it and made a beeline for the door. Curtis spoke up, "Young lady, excuse me, but I need to tell you that this young man is sweet on you."

I internally died a little bit. I turned every shade of red, laughed it off, and headed quickly out the door. Curtis got an earful from me when he got to the office, but he probably couldn't hear me through all his laughter.

Super inconveniently, I avoided the coffee shop for a few weeks, but eventually got the courage to walk back in there. Sure enough, there she was, looking at me with a slightly embarrassed and shy grin. I explained away the awkward old man; we had a good laugh, and I walked out the door with my coffee. I made it about a quarter mile down the road before I turned around and recognizing my own fear, I walked back in and asked her out to dinner.

The point of the story is that the same guy who told me not to date, told me when I was ready to date. I did not choose to reenter the dating world because of my impure thoughts or desperation to not be alone. Curtis, my counselor and friend, had a front row seat to all I had been doing with my life for the previous two years, and he influenced the decision when it was the right time.

Where there is no guidance, a people falls, but in an abundance of counselors there is safety.
—Proverbs 11:14

Without counsel plans fail, but with many advisors they succeed.
—Proverbs 15:22

The woman from the coffee shop and I dated for a few months, but it became clear that the Lord didn't intend for us to be together forever. When we broke up, it was the easiest breakup in my life—not that there were not feelings involved for both of us, but for the first time, I had been in a relationship with a woman that honored God. It was the first time I had worked to keep a relationship clean, and the lessons I gained from that would pay huge dividends in just a short time when I would eventually start dating the amazing woman God had picked to be my wife.

Let me add one piece of advice about dating that I received during this time. When I worked at the food warehouse, Tom Callahan and I would talk about dating in the future, and he told me that I should ask two questions of every girl I considered asking out:

- Do you love Jesus?
- What are you studying in God's word today?

The first question establishes that you are dating someone appropriate due to your faith. The second question tells you exponentially more about the person than the first. It tells you whether they are serious about their walk or are a Christian in name only. We need to know that we are yoking ourselves to someone who will challenge us spiritually, not just someone who grew up claiming the name of Jesus. There is no judgment in that question. If the person can't answer it, then maybe it is an opportunity to offer a suggestion. You will however gain a tremendous amount of foresight about your potential future in the answer. Last of all, you had better be prepared to answer that question yourself. If you cannot, then I would highly recommend you try dating Jesus a little before trying to date someone else.

Since renewing my commitment to Jesus that day in 2007, I have not made any major decisions in my life without first pursuing the safety of counselors. Today, as a leader at Miracle Hill and an ordained minister of the gospel, my secret sauce has not changed. Whenever faced with a decision, trial, or hardship, I connect myself to two things: the Lord and my mentors. I know that Ryan has historically made poor decisions when emotionally invested in a situation, so I eliminate myself from the equation. I know that when I can't figure out the right thing to do, the Lord will put someone in my path to help me discern His will and make the right decision.

Miracle Hill has used this approach for years to chart its path. Not only is the ministry guided by a group of committed humble servants in its board members, but the ministry also calls upon its staff to consider situations together in prayer. Our longtime former CEO, Reid modeled this over the years when faced with a trial, and the current leadership and I continue the practice.

If we do not know what to do with a situation, we call upon the whole ministry to gather physically or spiritually in prayer and fasting. We facilitate a time of prayer and listening to hear what each person hears the Lord telling us to do. I understand that I have been called to own the final decision and accompanying outcome, but it is a lot easier to feel confident in the voice of God when you are not the only person hearing Him.

A few years ago, we were trying to decide what to do with a recently emptied facility. We wound up with a list of ten or fifteen things that on the surface would all honor God and advance the mission and ministry of Miracle Hill. We worked through corporate prayer to whittle the list down to a couple of options, but none of us felt peace about any of the remaining options.

One day Tim Brown, our vice president of adult ministries, walked into my office and told me that the Lord had told another staff member and him that we needed to reconsider using the facility to expand our women's recovery efforts. That option had been taken off the list some weeks earlier. As I listened to him, I felt the Lord's peace rest in that decision. I spent the rest of the day talking and praying with the other leaders, and all of us felt the same way. The idea that had been removed based on man's attempt at good logic and reasoning was clearly the option the Lord wanted us to pursue and thus, Renewal Wade Hampton was born. This has been an amazing addition to the ministry for a few years, and it doubles our capacity to help women in recovery. I didn't come up with that idea, but the Lord certainly confirmed it through the prayers of many rather than the few.

Chapter 23

ALONE

Eventually, the time came for me to move out of the transitional housing community and into a less directed living environment. This is a necessary step on the path to independence, and those in recovery typically fall into one of two camps. Either they resent the need for transitional housing and its rules, or they are terrified of having to live life outside the safety net. The first group typically secretly desires to compromise in some way that transitional housing is preventing. Sure, they are living there by choice and can leave anytime they want, but often financial pressures or the desires of their family and friends influence them to stay in transition for some time beyond their personal desires. In many cases these individuals wind up hiding their compromise until the compromise exposes them in some way, forcing their hand. Some just leave under the cover of darkness.

The second group often desires to stay in residential care out of fear of the unknown. They believe that if they are in a Miracle Hill facility, then their walk and sobriety are guarded. Sometimes, these individuals have become institutionalized and their time in the safety net becomes counterproductive. They are resting in a false sense of security and inadvertently stop growing toward self-sufficiency.

There is a slim minority that truly progress to a place where they make a healthy decision to move on to the next phase of their journey. When it was time for me to move, I was in the fear-based group, scared to leave the nest. Yet I acknowledged that I needed to find some distance from the ministry in my personal life. I was working in the ministry, living in the ministry, and spending my evenings with ministry people at events and recovery groups. I knew it was time to take the next step, and I became excited to experience the next adventure that God had in store for my future.

I moved out of transition and into an apartment with two other recent graduates. We took on a lease in a nice apartment and flipped quarters to see who would get the master suite. Winner, winner chicken dinner for me.

In many cases freedom has a way of creating more problems than it solves for those in early recovery. Where a car is a huge blessing to those who do not have transportation, it also means that the world opens up around you and gives you more opportunities to do the wrong thing. Independent living does the same thing. Opportunity to make a compromise moves from the nearly impossible or at least inconvenient toward easy in the blink of an eye, or the rattle of a set of keys. While transitional housing allowed a tremendous amount of freedom, it was always in the back of my mind that I was under someone else's roof and liable to a drug and alcohol screen at any moment. This passive accountability is super effective for many of us.

We moved into the apartment and for a season experienced amazing growth. We went to church, meetings, and activities, not because we were told to, but because we wanted to. The Lord used our newfound freedom to show us that we could live successfully without such a firm hand guiding our every step. Having an apartment outside Miracle Hill also helped me to start seeing myself as successful from the world's perspective. I know that I should not define myself from the world's perspective, but this gave me fresh confidence in my situation that I was not living in a shelter or ministry housing. I was employed, housed, in college, and paying all my own bills. I was acting like an adult. As icing on the cake, when someone would ask what I was up to, I could look them in the eye and be proud of the man that the Lord was creating in me. I served Jesus for a living.

A few months into this independence, my roommates told me that they were going to Georgia for the weekend to visit family. I did not think anything of this and continued with my week. Friday, I got off work at my usual time and headed home. I remember walking into the apartment and instantly realizing that I was alone. I was alone in an apartment and could do whatever I wanted. The first thought that entered my head was, *"I can get drunk. I can drink tonight. I can drink tomorrow. I can sober up Saturday night and go to church on Sunday, and no one will ever know. No one will ever know."*

Wow. After a few years of growth and commitment while walking with the Lord, the first thought I had inside total freedom was to do the wrong thing. I remember standing there by the kitchen counter wrestling with my thoughts and my flesh. Here I was years later about to forget who I was. Praise the Lord I recognized I was close to disaster.

> *The heart is deceitful above all things, and desperately sick; who can understand it?*
> —Jeremiah 17:9

I immediately called one of my close friends, Matt, and we spent the weekend together. I surrounded myself with accountability and talked through the issue. I made it through the weekend and never acted on the thought. Jesus helped me to dodge a bullet.

I was so disappointed in myself for having the thought, but after further reflection, I became grateful that the Lord had given me clarity about the depth of my sin and the strength of my flesh. Even with all the progress in my life, the freedom of choice had given me an opportunity to choose wrong. And I was really close.

When we choose to do something wrong in our lives, we almost always do it in a vacuum. Sometimes, there is some outside pressure working to convince us to make the decision, but at the end of the day, I am the chief of sinners. It is me who is at fault. Owning and understanding this can go a long way toward convincing ourselves to take the hand off the wheel of life and let Jesus be the driver.

Recently, I was talking to an older gentleman early one morning at the gym when he asked me, "Are we who we think and say we are?" Very quickly I said no. We want to be perceived in a certain way and can convince others as well as ourselves that it is true. I told him that if my day starts with the realization that I am a broke, busted, and disgusted sinner saved by grace, then I am off to a good start. If I recognize my brokenness, then Jesus can help carve it away. If I want true peace each day, it has to be from the position of "there but for the grace of God go I."

A few more months went by in the apartment, and all was well. We all found our own individual rhythm in life, working and socializing, as our lives dictated. One day I realized that not one, but both my roommates had relapsed and were drinking. They could have been doing more, but I knew they were drinking for sure. Although they both have their own individual stories to tell, their concessions caught up with them, and their sobriety was compromised.

Talk about feeling alone. I was stuck in a lease with a couple of guys who were headed in a different direction than I was. I had a great relationship with both of them, but their decision seemed to lock me deeper into my commitment. We quickly found ourselves living as strangers in the same space. The lease ran its course in the next few months, and we went our separate ways.

Luckily, my buddy Matt was ready to move out of transitional housing, and we moved into a house in the heart of downtown. We lived so close to the city that at night or early in the morning, you could hear the lion's roar at the zoo from our front porch. Matt and I were quite different people, but our mutual commitment to walking out our recovery locked us into a healthy rhythm of life, and our friendship blossomed.

We have to find people with whom to do life. Like Simba and Puma, we each deeply need our own pack. Sometimes, the pack we choose has its challenges, but we were built for those challenges, and we are stronger because of them. We are strongest when we are not alone. Matt is and will always be my brother. Today his family and mine are close, and our children are growing up together.

Chapter 24

COUNSELING

T he life of a counselor at Miracle Hill—especially at the Overcomer Center, in my case—is not for the faint of heart. The day starts early with prayer and discussion about the day's activities, followed by three hours of group and several individual counseling sessions. In between all those activities is lesson planning, dealing with emergencies, interviewing prospective guests, and handling discipline issues. Some days, a situation will come up that railroads the rest of the day, and all those activities that you planned on doing have to be moved. If you are a person who loves task completion, this is not the job for you.

At Miracle Hill we would say that each staff member should have spiritual maturity commensurate with the position they hold. When I first moved over as a counselor at Overcomers, I certainly did not believe that I was mature enough to handle Scripture and discipleship at the level of the other experienced counselors, as these men were spiritual giants to me. I wanted what they had in life and was digging deep to understand the lessons the Lord teaches us through Scripture. I knew I was in a position of spiritual influence, and other than having a degree in the school of hard knocks, I was working twice as hard as everyone else to come up way short in the biblical understanding and interpretation department.

One day I walked into Bill Slocum's office with a question about Scripture. I believe it was some verse out of the Old Testament where I didn't understand its application. I had learned over the years not to come to Bill's office with a question unless I had done my homework. Bill would not just dish out knowledge unless he was fairly certain that you had prayed, researched, and sought the answer yourself. In this instance, I had done all these things and was still at an impasse.

I remember walking into his office and explaining my question to him. In my explanation I intentionally shared about the thoughtful time I had put into my own exploration so he would know that I had studied ahead of time. He listened intently to my question, thought for a moment, and reached behind himself for a Bible. As he started to read the passage, I walked around his desk to engage further in what he was doing.

That's when I realized that he had grabbed a Bible written in the original language, Hebrew. I sat down hard, dumbfounded at my own pride in thinking I had a good question, and asked, "You dumb yourself down to talk to me, don't you?"

Bill laughed it off and answered my original question about the text. Bill is a language scholar and deeply understands Hebrew and Greek in the context of Scripture. He is the smartest biblical scholar I know, and he chose to spend his career surrounded by immature Christians, agnostics, and atheists, ministering to their hearts. He could be teaching lectures at any seminary on the planet, but he chooses to serve. He could pastor or do anything he wants, but he chooses to lay his life out like a drink offering; so does his wife. Miracle Hill is filled with servants like Bill. I learned in that moment how deep the ministry rabbit hole goes and how shallow I was at that point in my walk. Although Bill is a Bible ninja due to his vast understanding of Scripture, the beauty of his relationship with the Lord is in the intimacy he has found with the

Lord. This didn't take him into the halls of some Bible institution, but deeper into submission to service. All these years later, I know that I am a little more mature and a little more educated than I was back then, but I am not Bill. I still very much want to be.

If you ask Bill what is most important, he will tell you people are. He will tell you that loving your neighbor is the most important thing in the world besides loving God.

> *And he said to him, "You shall love the Lord your God with all your heart and with all your soul and with all your mind. This is the great and first commandment. And a second is like it: You shall love your neighbor as yourself. On these two commandments depend all the Law and the Prophets."*
> —Matthew 22:37–40

Bill would agree with Jesus not because he has a command of the Scriptures, but because he is deeply in love with Jesus and over many years looks like Jesus. What a challenge to us all.

As a counselor, loving people proved to be the most important part of the job, and also the hardest. Every day I was interacting with men who were exactly like me in many ways and were in the trenches fighting the enemy at every step. Sometimes, guests act out due to the pain, and it is the counselor's job to be there to share in their trial. The ministry of presence is more important than knowing when and what to teach them.

One of the methods that Miracle Hill employs to promote understanding others is to encourage its staff to deeply understand themselves. We work hard to make sure that we are healthy and that we understand our own motivations, fears, and issues. That way, we can minister to others who have the same issues and reduce the risk of transferring their garbage onto ourselves, or ours onto them.

Bill was a big fan of personality profiling used as a tool to help understand oneself. He was a certified trainer and eventually tested me.

Through that experience I learned a lot about myself, but also learned about Bill. He shared that he was wired similarly to me and was more comfortable with being analytical and task oriented. While I believed him, I was also confused because he had always been one of the most relational people I knew. What he was telling me was that he is not naturally geared to be relational, so he has to compensate for his lack of relational desire. He knew that Jesus was relational and because he wanted to be like Jesus, he worked hard at it. In fact, I learned that he used a trick.

Because Bill was task oriented, he turned being relational into a task. Every morning, he put a stack of quarters on one side of his desk. Every time he initiated something relational, he would move a quarter to the other side of the desk. His goal was to move the entire stack by the end of the day. He was gaming the system literally to eliminate his own shortcomings for Jesus's sake.

One afternoon, several months after I learned this, I walked by Bill in the main hall at the Greenville Rescue Mission. He stopped me in the hall, gave me a big hug, and then gushed with some encouragement directed at me. I walked away from the encounter feeling a little lighter and more optimistic about my day. I walked all the way back to my office before the reality of what had just transpired dawned on me. I quickly walked back, entered his office, and asked, "Was I just a quarter?"

Bill just smiled and said something else encouraging, but I was on to him. After that day, recognizing how much that one little interaction affected my emotions, I put my own stack of quarters on the desk. There is nothing disingenuous about the stack of quarters. Neither Bill nor I move the quarters to check a box; we move the quarters to be like Jesus.

Rick Sholette was one of my counselors the first time I went through Overcomers, and he taught me potentially the most important aspect of being a counselor. He was a licensed professional counselor outside of his work with Miracle Hill and has a counseling practice called Paraclete Ministries. *Paraclete* is a Greek word found in the Johannine texts and is descriptive of for the Holy Spirit; we often translate it as helper or counselor. The actual meaning of the word *parakletos* is "one called to the side of another."

Rick would say that this is what we are called to do, come alongside someone. We do so not out of a position of authority but of equality as each of us is made in the image of God and a sinner in need of a savior whether we realize it or not. The fundamental nature of what Miracle Hill's counselors do is found in the essence of this word. They get down in the dirt with our guests and help them determine how they are going to dig their way out of the hole they are in. Sometimes, they just sit in the dirt together.

The problems the counselors face are as diverse as the guests. They deal with traumas, family brokenness, poor decision-making, medical emergencies, suicidal ideation, and drug overdoses. They wipe tears with the sleeves of their clean shirts and shed tears quietly. They counsel parents and diffuse crisis situations. They are truly Jesus to the world, and they do it day after day after day.

I remember the first time that somebody I was counseling died. He was probably just a few years younger than me and was on my caseload for only a few months. One day he decided to leave the program. I used every tactic I knew to try to talk him into staying, but eventually he packed up his belongings and left the shelter. A few days later, he was found dead, of an overdose. As is often the case, he was found days after the overdose which means he was either isolated at the time of his death or had been abandoned by whomever he was with. He was alone in death as he perceived he was alone in life, and it maddened me that he didn't have to be.

I was shattered. I was grieving, but I was also mad at the senselessness of the situation. On top of that I felt guilty that I had not tried harder to help him or said the right thing to keep him from leaving. In my grief I made my way to Bill's office for my own counseling session. Bill sat quietly with me and listened to me grieve and cry and yell. He sat quietly while I tried to rationalize the death. He just sat with me quietly listening and being present. Again, the best counselors are all great listeners. Eventually, the tears started to dry up, and he looked at me and said, "Ryan if you are going to take credit for the failures, then you have to take credit for the successes. Since God gets credit for the successes, who are you to take credit for the failures?"

He put my job and the job of every counselor into perspective in one sentence. Our job is not to fix anyone. We are to present the truth of the gospel. We are to plant. We are to water. God grants the increase. Or He doesn't. That is entirely His business, and we are just tools He chooses to use along the way.

We are present in the heart of the storm and comfort in the midst of tragedy. We present truth when appropriate but lead with love and relationship. We come alongside and stick when the going gets tough. What a cool and humbling job.

As the years go by our counselors have become more effective and skilled by the world's standards. They have increased training opportunities, and the walls of their offices have more plaques and degrees. The essence of what they do remains the same. They come alongside the broken and brokenhearted and love them like they love God.

Chapter 25

WYATT

Checking into the mission in 2003, I was initially assigned to be on the house crew as my daily task assignment. Miracle Hill helps every guest to understand personal discipline and ownership. Residential guests are typically assigned to have some chore or task for which they are responsible each day. Guests cook the meals in the kitchen and drive the vans. They mop their own dorms and wash sheets in the laundry. Those assigned to the house crew are responsible for cleaning the mission from tip to stern and taking care of the landscaping. When I showed up for work the first day, I met my new boss, Wyatt who was a longtime shelter resident and had been in and out of the mission for over twenty years when I met him. He would check into the mission, find stability emotionally and spiritually, get a job, move out, and return to the mission within a year. With no exaggeration, he probably did this twenty times over those twenty-plus years and spent over half his adult life living in institutions.

Wyatt was not nice to most people. He was mean as a rattlesnake to those he didn't know and trust, but I quickly learned there was a softer side to Wyatt. The first day he was very direct with me on what I needed to do and how I needed to do it. Although still foggy from withdrawal,

I desired his approval and worked hard to do what he told me to do. By the end of the week, he told me that I did a good job, not something that easily came out of his mouth. Within a month, Wyatt was my friend. He was at least twice my age and while I was looking for people to look up to, Wyatt was looking for people he could trust. He needed people as much as all of us do, but in his brokenness, he had created a forcefield to keep everyone away. His defense mechanism was his abrupt and direct personality paired with a short fuse on his temper.

As the weeks went by and I earned Wyatt's trust, he and I would finish a task and then go to his office, an old, donated desk at the back of a storage closet. We would sit back there and drink stale overcooked coffee and talk. Wyatt was one of those guys who knew a lot about everything—a jack of all trades. If he got to know you, then he loved to share his knowledge of the world with you. When I think of him, I think of a mustached, street-hardened version of Dwight Schrute from *The Office*. He worked hard in all that he did and had a great relationship with the staff. Many people may have seen Wyatt as someone to shy away from, someone not worth their time, but I saw a man who deeply wanted love in his life. He just didn't know how to let anyone in.

I regularly found myself defending Wyatt with the other guests. Often people would be upset with him because he was a rule follower and was in a position to be a rule enforcer. When Wyatt was in the shelter, he was quickly entrusted with the daily operation of all sorts of mission tasks. Wyatt knew he was valued and had purpose when he was in the mission, and it showed in how he lived his life.

Once I graduated from Overcomers and was in the servant leadership program, Wyatt and I had two tiny one-room apartments directly beside each other above the gym and kitchen of the mission. Strangely, even though Wyatt was in his fifties, he had a mild obsession with video games. I think Wyatt was using the video games in the same way that addicts use drugs, to escape. Also, it gave him a puzzle to solve that was far easier than life itself. When the going got tough, he could just shut it off. Sometimes, a stay in a shelter does the same thing for our guests; it allows them to quiet the noise from the world for a season and turn off the console until they are ready to play the game again.

In the evenings I would go into his room, and we would play whatever game system he had gotten his hands on. Mostly he would play, and I would watch. Wyatt would spend hours showing me all the cool things he had figured out or accomplished in one game or another. It was an escape, but Wyatt was alive in those moments, able to handle the world he was immersed in. He could talk endlessly about the goals of each game, excited to have some aspect of life in which he perceived that he had total control. Control was another illusion in his life.

Over the course of his journey with Miracle Hill, he became a staff member two or three times. Each time his attitude and temper would eventually become an issue, and he would get fired or unexpectedly quit. No one would see him for a few months, and then he would check back into the mission a little older and more worn down than the time before.

When I eventually went to work for Miracle Hill, years after our nightly video game sessions in those tiny one-room apartments, Wyatt was on another rotation at the mission. One day I was working at the food warehouse and Wyatt came strolling over to me; he had been rehired by Jim Wolff to sort donated goods at the warehouse. His job was to take these giant boxes of electronics and knick-knacks and determine what was good, what was bad, and what needed to be fixed. This was a puzzle Wyatt excelled at. Each day he would work tirelessly resurrecting old record players, televisions, and kids' toys. His work area was immaculate and organized, and you would not find a person better suited to this position. Over the next year, I saw Wyatt nearly every day. He walked into the food warehouse frequently to share some bit of information he had learned or to show me some gadget he had fixed. He was a great asset to the warehouse, eventually moving out of the mission and into an apartment.

One day after work I went over to Wyatt's apartment to see where he had moved and how he was adjusting. I walked into this low-income apartment and was immediately face to face with a wall of electronics. Wyatt had every game system you could imagine and an expensive TV and sound system at its center. My initial reaction was to remind him what neighborhood he was in and to tell him not to show this to anyone, or he would most certainly be robbed.

He didn't have a car. He didn't have many relationships. Wyatt was comfortable in all the wrong ways in that apartment. He was completely isolated from the world, but thought he was living like a king.

When I changed jobs and moved back to the mission as a counselor, I saw Wyatt less often. Once every couple of weeks, I would have some reason to be at the warehouse and would make a point to stop by and see him. He would be in his own world, fixing some piece of furniture or electronic device, and we would have a short conversation. I always encouraged him to get more involved in some activity or church, but I was his peer and his friend, not his boss. He would curtly give me one excuse or another and go back to his workbench. I would laugh it off and head back to my day. He also began relationally separating himself from me. As our frequency of interactions lessened, his trust waned. His needs relationally were centered on those he saw frequently. I believe this represented safety to him.

One day I found out that Wyatt had yelled at a bunch of people at work and had stormed out. He didn't come back to work after that, but I expected that in a few short months, he would check back into the mission.

A few months later his landlord went to check on him because he was extremely late on paying his rent. They found him hanging in the shower. Dead and alone. Wyatt had lived his life alone, and Wyatt died alone, believing he had no other options. I had the honor of preaching his memorial service at the rescue mission. There were only a few people there—almost exclusively mission guests and staff.

The reality is that there are hundreds of Wyatts at Miracle Hill. Wyatt didn't have a severe mental illness or an inability to work.

Wyatt's life had led him to a place where he was probably marginally institutionalized; he was very reluctant to trust anyone, and he struggled with relationships. He had developed a strong fight-or-flight defense mechanism. If the going got tough in Wyatt's life, Wyatt got going.

I believe that the difference for Wyatt of when he was healthy and when he wasn't was community. When he was deeply imbedded into the life of the mission, he had purpose. During these times, he went to church and was occasionally pleasant to others. This helped him to get employment opportunities, which led to success as defined by the world. Once he achieved that success, he would wake up and be alone. He wouldn't have people around him to tell him that they cared for him, whether he wanted them to or not. The other guests and things that he would gripe and complain about at the mission were probably the things that helped him to stay well and stay alive.

When people see someone experiencing homelessness on the side of the road, old-school philosophy would prompt them to think: "He needs to go get a job." For Wyatt and others, that isn't the answer to the problems of their lives. Wyatt needed community—not forced, but so readily available that it was impossible to ignore. He needed to not be able to accidentally hide from the world. He needed someone who would love him whether he liked it or not and would engage with him even when he didn't want them to. Does that sound like someone you know?

In the Gospel of John, what is Jesus's first act after baptism? He begins to call the disciples and create community. He could have done anything to proclaim his ministry and to start things off with a bang. Instead, the Son of man calls broken men into fellowship. The God of the universe spent His time on earth showing us how we should love and live. He did that intimately in community.

Bear one another's burdens, and so fulfill the law of Christ.
—Galatians 6:2

I don't think that the mission should be a permanent place for anyone to live, but we need to wrestle with the reality for people like Wyatt. How do we marry the idea of community with a permanent living situation? Where should Wyatt have been?

I believe that if we had some type of efficiency apartment that Wyatt could have lived in, where there was someone to say hello to him every day when he got home, Wyatt's story might have been different. Over the years I have seen hundreds of guests come through and be successful, and I have seen hundreds leave and die. Many of them are just like Wyatt.

All of us need community in our lives. We need people who care about us despite our own efforts to shove them away. Modern thinking about the issue of homelessness would desire to put someone into a house quickly to solve their problems. How does a house help when the problems they experience are inside themselves?

Shouldn't the church offer some type of solution if the ministry of community and presence was defined by its creator? Who went to visit Wyatt when he was alone? I confess that I did not. I knew where he was, and I knew his tendency toward isolation, but I let busyness keep me from pursuing him. I only confess this because I want to do better. God wants us all to do better.

The family is the foundational institution of our society and is constituted by marriage, blood, or adoption. It is ordained by God Himself. With Wyatt's confession of faith, he was my brother, and if you are a believer, he was your brother as well. Sure, he was hard to love at times, but so am I and so are you.

Every one of us knows someone like Wyatt. With the period at the end of this sentence, put down the book and pick up your phone.

Chapter 26

CLAWSON THE LOBSTER

Although Overcomers is an amazing place to find Jesus and get your life on track, it can also be filled with tremendous amounts of drama and chaos. This is true for all of our residentially set programs and shelters. When you put dozens of hurting people in the same room, you are inviting a little tension to enter the mix. Hurt people tend to, well, hurt people.

The tension can be a really good thing, as the stirred pot allows people to work through their garbage in real time. Sometimes, the tension can boil over, and the staff have to be ready to respond at a moment's notice to one situation or another.

Today, Overcomers has its own campus, but during my time in the program and during my initial years as a counselor, the program was located in the Greenville Rescue Mission. The rescue mission was a congregate living facility which, at full capacity, had sixty men living side by side in one big bunk-filled room. At night, a chorus of snores and flatulence caused the room to sound and smell like a jungle.

Each man was responsible to keep his area tidy, and everyone was responsible for the cleanliness of the dorm. The consequence for not holding up your end of the equation was to receive a demerit. Do you remember referrals from school? Demerits were essentially referrals from school except they were for grown folk instead of toddlers. Behaviorally, there often isn't a significant difference between those two populations. Essentially, the purpose of a demerit was to make the person think and answer a few key questions:

- Why did you get this demerit?
- What can you do to prevent getting a demerit like this again?
- What did you learn from this?
- What Scripture applies to this?

The demerit itself did not have a lot of weight other than inconvenience, but the guests treated a demerit as a potentially life-altering judgment on their life. Certainly, it could turn into a bigger deal if the man did not take it seriously. A heap of demerits would result in a write-up, and a write-up could be a very big deal. Sometimes, big deals start off as a very small thing.

One day in 2008 or 2009, a group of guys left the mission to go to work at the warehouse as part of their daily chores. Their job was to pack unsellable clothes into a bailing machine so that those thousand-pound bales could be sold overseas. One of the guys came across a tiny red Beanie Baby lobster named Clawson among the clothes, and he decided to put the lobster in his pocket to bring it back to the mission.

Once he returned to the dorm, he thought it would be funny to put Clawson partly under his new bunkmate's comforter, so that only Clawson's head and claws were sticking out. He knew that his bunkmate would get a demerit for having a stuffed animal. He was thinking of his own status in the dorm, believing a simple prank would be well-received and hilarious in the eyes of his friends.

Once the lobster was placed and with perfect timing, the team leader came through for a dorm inspection, spotted Clawson, confiscated Clawson, and wrote a demerit for the new guy. His bunkmate was across the dorm watching this scene develop and was bragging to his friends while laughing hysterically.

Eventually, the new guy returned from his pre-program class and saw the demerit. Not being in on the joke at his expense, he started asking people why he had gotten the demerit. Since there is no honor among thieves and no one wanted to get the blame, several people immediately told the man who was responsible. He looked around, and his bunkmate was nowhere to be found.

Within minutes the man saw his bunkmate hiding outside by one of the trees in the yard. Without saying a word, he walked directly out to the jokester. The air was thick with tension as everyone watched the impending altercation with great interest. As the man approached, the jokester smiled and began explaining away his crime. Without saying a word or breaking his stride, the new guy swung and landed a punch that thankfully knocked his bunkmate out cold while shattering his nose. The joke lost its humor immediately to all who were in on it. The new guy just looked down at the jokester for a moment or two while everyone around them stood frozen. Then he dropped the screwdriver that was tucked into his other hand, strolled over to the fence, hopped it, and walked away. To my knowledge no one ever saw the victim-turned-attacker again.

What the mischief-maker didn't know is that his new bunkmate had just finished a twenty-year sentence in prison. The one unpardonable rule of prison life is that you do not, under any circumstances, touch another man's belongings. The screwdriver was meant to end his life, over a lobster, but his weak chin saved his life. When he decided to steal the lobster and make the joke, I am sure it seemed like a very small thing, but the little things in life matter.

One who is faithful in a very little is also faithful in much, and one who is dishonest in a very little is also dishonest in much.

—Luke 16:10

Today Clawson lives in my office. I have taught dozens of classes with Clawson as the illustration, but his purpose is more of a reminder to me than anybody else.

In my life, nearly every bad thing that was big started with a bad thing that was small. Certainly, that is true for my story of addiction and relapse, but it extends to other failures as well. Sometimes, the small thing was an exception to a rule that I gave myself permission to ignore, thinking, *"Perhaps I can do it this one time. It won't be a big deal if no one finds out."*

Sometimes, nothing bad happens after that decision, but other times it does. In all my years of talking to others about their brokenness, I have yet to hear someone say that they started out with the intention of having their life fall into destruction. Most woke up one day and looked around only to find that the little failures outweighed the little successes by a lot. They didn't even see it happening, but over time the little things added up. One moment, you are breathing clearly and the next, your head is covered, and water is choking your lungs.

A common tool taught at Miracle Hill to help with this dilemma is the idea of taking a daily inventory of your life. The idea is that you take stock of what you are doing with regularity to make yourself aware of the justifications, rationalizations, and poor decisions you have made over the course of a day.

I read an article that said that successful people have two things in common. Most make goals for their life, and most journal or keep a diary. One of those tasks points toward the future, and the other keeps a tally on the past. Journaling is just another way to intentionally inventory your life.

We destroy arguments and every lofty opinion raised against the knowledge of God, and take every thought captive to obey Christ.
—2 Corinthians 10:5

When I started going to church, I really struggled to keep focused in the service when I was praying. My mind would be flooded with random thoughts, often horrible thoughts, not meant for a time of prayer. I came across this passage in 2 Corinthians and decided to try to do what the passage said. For the next few months, every time I found myself being distracted when I was trying to pray, I would write down the thought that entered my mind. Then I would return to my prayer. If it happened again, I would write it down again. I did this over and over as many times as it took to get through the prayer. At the end of the day, I would journal, and then I would confess the thoughts that I had and ask God to remove them. Over time, God began to do just that. Eventually, I found that I could pray for longer periods of time. Sometimes, through this process God shows me areas of my life where I needed counseling or areas where I needed to talk through an issue with a Christian brother.

Essentially, what I am describing is confession and repentance. We cannot, however, repent from areas of our lives that we do not see or are not aware of. Without awareness, the little things begin to rule, and we risk the tidal wave to come.

Through awareness, confession, and repentance, the little things that so easily beset us don't stand a chance. Add some accountability into the mix, and the enemy can't find a spot to get a foothold in our life.

It is for discipline that you have to endure. God is treating you as sons. For what son is there whom his father does not discipline? . . . For the moment all discipline seems painful

rather than pleasant, but later it yields the peaceful fruit of
righteousness to those who have been trained by it.
—Hebrews 12:7, 11

This isn't supposed to be easy, but it is simple. Look at your life, find the broken places, invite Jesus in to wash you, and one day you will wake up with your life reflecting Him in a way that you never imagined. It can be painful to develop the discipline necessary to not let the little things overwhelm you, but it is eternally worth it, and it is what God calls each of us to do. We are not called to the sideline to watch Jesus run the race, but to run it with Him. If we don't keep the house clean through regular inventory, there are hilarious little Clawsons waiting in our future to help us get shanked by a screwdriver. In my opinion, the choice is easy.

This story started with the idea that hurt people hurt people. The inverse of that is true as well. Loved people love people. The more we are loved, the more we can pour out love. We do this one little thing at a time. Imagine a world where we build the discipline to love one another well. What if instead of finding ways to slowly dig our own graves, we worked every day to find some small way to love the people around us?

Clawson the lobster is neither good nor evil. He is an inanimate object to be used at our discretion. How we choose to use the Clawsons in our lives is what makes all the difference.

Chapter 27

SALVATION, ACT II

C ounseling at Miracle Hill requires you to develop expertise in various tasks needed to help the program or mission operate. Not only do they counsel people assigned to their caseload, but counselors teach classes, make task rosters, and do a variety of administrative tasks. Counselors have to deal with discipline issues and drug tests and every other imaginable task involved in running a residential facility. One of the elements that I felt particularly unprepared for was the evangelistic element of the job. Be clear that Miracle Hill exists to help people who are experiencing homelessness and to tell them about Jesus. I was clearly supposed to be Jesus to those that I interacted with, but I also needed to have enough command of Scripture to share the gospel with them and help them wrestle through the truths of Scripture—the same as was done for me.

To prepare for this portion of the job, I studied a great deal, and over time my ability to connect to the living word of God became less robotic when I talked with guests. I memorized the Romans Road and waited for an opportunity to help someone walk down it.

One day a very young man who was a recent intake into the program stopped by my office to ask a few questions. He wasn't on my caseload, but I knew who he was, and because my office was inside the dorm, I often experienced opportunities with men that I otherwise wouldn't interact with. Aiden was eighteen years old, had a mild learning disability, and had the maturity level of a young teen. He had bounced in and out of group homes for most of his youth and was desperate to find somewhere on this planet that he felt like he belonged.

We began talking and very quickly, it became apparent to me that Aiden was ripe for the gospel and was nearly ready to make a life-altering decision. Nervousness filled me as I knew this was an opportunity ordained by God to be Jesus to this young man, and hopefully the Lord would use me to help him understand salvation. As we continued talking, I began walking him down the Romans Road.

"Aiden, do you know that all of us are broken sinners? Romans 3:10 tells us that '*there is no one righteous, not even one,*' and Romans 3:23 says that '*all have sinned and fall short of the glory of God.*'"

"Yes," Aiden replied. "I realize that my life is a mess, and I make a mess of everything. That's why I am here."

I continued further along the Romans way. "If God is who He says He is and we sin against Him, what kind of outcome do we receive?" I paused and then added, "Romans goes on to show that if this is true, then the outcome is our own destruction, payment for our crimes. Romans 6:23 says that the '*wages of sin in death.*'"

Aiden said, "I get it. If anyone deserves death for the things, they have done, it is me. I have messed up so much in my life and can't seem to get right."

I reassured him. "Wait a minute, there is good news in the midst of this; the verse goes on to say that the '*gift of God is eternal life in Christ Jesus.*' We can have hope because Jesus knew this about us, you and me. He knew that we were sinners, and Romans 5:8 tells us that God demonstrates His own love for us in that while He knew *'we were still sinners, Jesus died for us.'* Isn't that amazing?"

Aiden sat deep in thought but remained silent.

I plunged ahead: "Jesus loves you so much that He went to the cross for you, in your brokenness, in your sin. Brother, I am just as broken as you and have messed up so much, but Jesus. He died for me anyway because God knew we couldn't be righteous on our own."

Finally, Aiden spoke again: "This is crazy. Why would he love me? I am a worthless man."

"I know it's crazy, but He loves you because he created you. He doesn't think you are worthless; He believes you are valuable. Aiden, He made you in His image. He gave you free will knowing that you would make stupid decisions, but He also knew that all that worked to find you in this moment, right here, right now. He loves you so much and made sure that you would be presented with the truth. He made sure you would understand who Jesus really is and have an opportunity to respond to it. Jesus is so good to us and knows we are hardheaded, so He put the instructions of what we should do right in His book. Romans 10:9–10 says if you declare *'with your mouth that Jesus is Lord and believe in your heart that God raised him from the dead, you will be saved.'* The next verse says that it is with your mouth that you profess your faith and are saved. All we have to do is acknowledge who He is and ask him to be Lord of our life, not just savior but Lord also. That's it."

Aiden exclaimed, "Not me. I have done too much."

"Yes, you. His word says that *'all have fallen short,'* but Romans 10:13 says that everyone—**everyone**—who calls on the name of the Lord will be saved. If you do that, what do you get? Exactly what you have been looking for and didn't know it: peace and joy. Romans 5:1–2 says that as we are justified through faith in Jesus, '*we have peace with God.*' Then it says that through Jesus, we gain access into His grace. Don't you want peace and joy and to receive His grace for your life?"

"Yes," Aiden answered softly.

"On top of that, guilt goes away. Romans 8:1 says that for those who believe, there is no longer any condemnation. That's a fancy way of saying that you are no longer guilty. Jesus paid your debt on the cross, and your sin is no longer yours to bear. Do you want that—freedom from guilt?

"Yes," Aiden whispered.

"If you want it, you can have it. We can pray together right now, I will lead you word for word, and you can start living a new life with Jesus by your side. Do you want that?

Now sobbing, Aiden said, "Yes, I really do."

"Do you want me to show you how to pray?"

Aiden continued sobbing as he answered, "Yes."

"I'll say a line and then you repeat it as best you can, OK?"

Aiden nodded his head and then, line by line, he repeated this prayer of salvation after me:

God, I know that I am a sinner.

I know that because of my sin, I deserve death and hell.

I believe that you sent Jesus, your Son, as a payment for my sin.

I declare Jesus as Lord of my life and believe that my faith for salvation is through the death and resurrection of Jesus.

Thank you for saving me a sinner. Amen!

So, Aiden was saved, and I was over the moon. I cannot describe the level of excitement I experienced or how fulfilled I felt from having a new brother. My shift at work was ending and I went home to bask in the reality of what I had just experienced. I slept really well that night.

The next day I showed up to work standing a little bit taller and feeling pretty good about myself. I walked through the building and entered my office right about the time that one of the other guys came up to me and asked me if I had heard the good news. Aiden had gotten saved.

With a big smile on my face, I told him that I had heard the good news. Another guy chirped in and said, "Yeah, Aiden got saved last night in chapel."

The first guy interjected, "No, he didn't; he got saved last night on the volleyball court after the game. He prayed with a few of us."

A third guy from across the dorm, "No, you two got it wrong, Aiden prayed with a volunteer last night after the pre-program Bible study."

My smile dropped.

Honestly, I was offended. I had poured out all the wisdom I knew on this boy, and he felt that he needed more from others. Did this mean that what had happened between us wasn't good enough for him?

Truthfully, Aiden was so excited about meeting the Lord that he had prayed the sinner's prayer a half dozen times in the previous twelve hours. He was desperate to make it stick and did whatever he had to do to ensure that it was real.

That evening Jesus took me to the woodshed. He showed me that Aiden's salvation had nothing to do with me or anything I had to say. God alone is the author of our fate.

For there is one God, and there is one mediator between God and men, the man Christ Jesus, who gave himself as a ransom for all, which is the testimony given at the proper time.
—1 Timothy 2:5–6

I can certainly present the truth of the Scripture and lead someone down the road, but God determines if they pass go and collect two hundred dollars. Salvation is not something I can spiritually wield as a weapon to cut the devil out of someone else's life. It just simply is not ours to give.

So, when did Aiden meet Jesus? I have no idea if he did then or if he ever did. A few months later Aiden returned to the streets and left Overcomers in his rear view. If I ever meet Aiden in heaven, then I guess I will get an answer. Certainly, it will not matter when it happened. In retrospect, I did my job. I believe I was open to the leading of the Holy Spirit, I shared the gospel, and God will do what He wants with that. I don't have to worry about the outcome because the relationship is between the person and their maker. I have little to nothing to do with the equation. Faithfulness to share truth is what Jesus is after in my life and yours. He doesn't care if we are articulate or if we bumble through our words. He cares that we are willing to share the words at all.

Over the years I have had a few dozen opportunities to walk someone down the Romans Road or to explain the gift of salvation through simpler means. Sometimes they pray a prayer, but often they don't. Sometimes, I get to see God working miracles in their life, but often they go back to the idols and broken places, content in counterfeit peace for another season. I rest in the reality that God's word, His truth, can and will do more for their life than I ever could.

I find that sharing the gospel is one of the more challenging aspects of walking with the Lord. Comparatively, it is much easier to walk with Jesus than to tell a stranger the truth of the Scriptures. It is even harder to share it with a family member or someone we know. However, God's word is clear, and it is something we must do. In His word we can rest. Our words do not have to be eloquent. We just have to be willing, and God will work out the rest.

For the word of God is living and active, sharper than any two-edged sword, piercing to the division of soul and of spirit, of joints and of marrow, and discerning the thoughts and intentions of the heart. And no creature is hidden from his sight, but all are naked and exposed to the eyes of him to whom we must give account.

—Hebrews 4:12–13

Chapter 28

GIFT

When I am healthy, I tend to focus on the areas of my life about which I am passionate. In my early recovery years, I was mostly focused on Jesus, ministry, college, physical health, community, and more Jesus. To cope with the chaos in my life and in opposition to who I once was, I turned my life into a rigid schedule of activities each day. The first few years, I penciled in my ministry responsibilities, school activities, and church activities, and then I tried to find time for other things. Given the busyness of my life, there was not a lot of time for other activities.

My roommate Matt and I were like passing ships in the night as he and I had our own lives and schedules. Friday was typically guys night, which meant pepperoni and bacon pizza and some bad action movie. In December of 2008, I made a new year's resolution to not watch TV for a year to see what I could accomplish without the distraction. Within a few months, I saw a huge benefit from this and found more time for other things in my life.

During this time, my church followed a traditional approach to services, and most of us were there whenever the doors were open: Sunday morning, Sunday evening, and Wednesday evening minimally.

I also started attending a variety of social gatherings with my new church family. Soon after becoming a member of the church, I became part of a multigenerational friend group, and I found myself saying no to activities, not because I did not want to go, but because I got so many offers. It was amazing to feel welcomed and wanted.

My friend group grew, and I found friendships at church in nearly every age group. I often said no to events that I thought included only young people, but yes to events that I perceived as multigenerational.

One couple at church, Ray and Peggy White, usually had cookouts at their farm around the holidays, and many from our church would attend. We would drive out into the country to shoot fireworks for the Fourth of July or carve pumpkins in the fall. The Whites' daughter, Lauren, was beautiful and fierce but was almost ten years younger than me. I remember numerous conversations with my buddies talking about how beautiful she was and how they wanted to date her.

I had noticed her the first Sunday evening that I attended Rocky Creek Church. When the choir got up on stage, my eyes found this beautiful raven-haired girl in the front row; I was mesmerized watching a young woman caught up in unabashed worship. I later learned her name was Lauren White; she was truly stunning.

Lauren and I had an interesting relationship for a few years. She dated one of my friends, and I had a lot of interaction with her through church, social outings, and cookouts at her parents' farm. If you asked her about this period, she would tell you that she thought I was stuck up, disagreeable, hard to get to know, and that I would ask extremely hard questions of her and her friends. I thought she was young and naïve, and because she was a sixth or seventh generation member of the church, I saw her as royal, a church princess if you will, and untouchable.

Regardless of how we felt about each other, we were stuck in each other's orbits for reasons that only God knew.

After a few cookouts at the farm one summer, I found myself in a conversation with Peggy about their horses, which were being used as pasture ornaments at the time. I jokingly berated her for wasting those beautiful animals, and she would give it back to me, talking about what it takes to run a farm.

One day Ray and Peggy took in two large, beautiful quarter horses named Winston and Vader. Winston was dark brown with a white streak down his nose, and Vader was as you probably guessed, jet black. They had been rescued from an abusive situation and stood fifteen or sixteen hands. I don't exactly know what that means, but they were big. Real big.

Within a few weeks, there was another cookout at the farm, and I got to meet these new horses as we fed them carrots one evening. I looked at Peggy and asked, "What are you going to do with these two? Waste them like the others?"

Peggy retorted, "Those two horses are unbroken. If you don't want them wasted, someone needs to break them. What are you going to do, Ryan Duerk, break 'em?"

Now I do not know a thing about horses. I am a city boy who grew up in suburbia. I have never spent time around farm animals or horses other than getting on the back of one at a fair and riding in a circle when I was a toddler, but I was younger than I am now and dumb so I said, "Yes, I will." Peggy laughed out loud.

Over the following weeks and months, I began going to the farm a couple of times a week to join Ray and his father Bill as they worked with these two horses. In time, we worked up to getting a saddle on them and began slowly riding around the round pen, and then outside the round pen. Were they broken? Not exactly. For the most part, they tolerated us and allowed us to sit on their backs. We never worked the horses toward being neck reigned, but the experience was amazing, nonetheless.

I thought I was at the farm to work with the horses, but God had other plans. As I worked with the horses, I also spent a lot of time with Lauren. When I got bucked off Winston in the round pen, she was there to make sure I was OK and then to laugh at me hysterically. When we were freezing in the middle of winter, Lauren and her mom brought us coffee and a homemade biscuit to warm up. When it started to get dark early as it does in the winter, we would retreat to her parents' home for food and fellowship. I found myself doing my homework in their living room, playing Wii games with Lauren, and finding the comfort of family in the process.

Although I had become healthy in many areas of my life, I was still dealing with the garbage in my head about who I was, what I deserved, and what God wanted for me. I genuinely thought that Lauren was too young for me, did not have enough life experience, and could not possibly understand who I was or where I had been. I believed deeply that I would wind up with another person in recovery. Not that there is anything wrong with that, as I know many married couples in recovery who are super successful and who are chasing Jesus, but my motivation was based on my understanding of my brokenness rather than my worth in Christ.

One day Lauren and I had a conversation at a Starbucks. Before we met that day, I was very intentional to tell her, like a jerk, that it was not a date. She says that I called it a friendly meeting. Over a cup of coffee Lauren expressed a desire for us to date. I directly laid out all my reasons why we could not see each other romantically. But she did not care about the reasons I had concocted in my head and told me that we were, in fact, going to date and that I was wrong. She saw Jesus in me rather than my past and did not have as much interference hearing from Jesus as I did. Let it not be lost on you that I was who I was, and she knew it. She would have to explain to her family and friends that she was going to date a former criminal who was almost a decade older. But she cared more about what God was telling her than anyone else.

The Lord took me back to the woodshed over the next few weeks and told me to get over myself. He had clearly shown me through the experiences of the past year that Lauren was exactly who He wanted me to chase Him with, and I needed to be obedient and quit letting my insecurities get in the way.

In December of 2009 I called Ray and asked him if I could have permission to ask Lauren out on a date. He said yes, so I hung up and called Lauren asking her if I could take her out to dinner for her birthday in a few weeks. On Friday, January 15th, Lauren's birthday, we had our first date. By March 15th of that same year, I said to Lauren, "I don't know what else I need to know about you in order to know that we are supposed to be together forever." She agreed, and I knew that she was the one.

Monday, September 6th, the Whites had another cookout at the farm, and what Lauren did not know is that I had already talked to her dad, and I had a plan. At the end of the night, I got a bag of carrots out for Lauren and me to feed the horses. On the way up, there was a box containing two plugs that I asked Lauren to connect, and the round pen was immediately illuminated in Christmas lights. We were back to where we started. I asked her to be my wife, and she agreed. We were married on March 19, 2011.

There is no way I could have written the story God had for my marriage. He always knows what is best for us and who is best for us. As is the theme for much of my story, God's choice was not on my radar, but He led me exactly where He wanted me.

A few years ago, Lauren and I moved to the farm, purchasing her parents' house from them. We have two beautiful children who are growing up on this amazing piece of property surrounded by a family who loves them. My kids hear about Jesus every day and fight about who gets to pray at dinner. The life God has built for me far surpasses the one I thought I could build for myself.

He always knows better because He loves us way more than we love ourselves. He does not promise life will be easy, but it is good, always good, when you live in His economy. In it, He delivers a continual flow of real peace with heaping piles of goodness in our lives.

Now to him who is able to do far more abundantly than all that we ask or think, according to the power at work within us, to him be glory in the church and in Christ Jesus throughout all generations, forever and ever. Amen.
—Ephesians 3:20–21

After many years of marriage, I can tell you that Lauren was not just a good pick for me. She was handpicked by the creator of the universe for me. She is kind. She is thoughtful. She is still fierce and brave. She is tender with our children and direct when she needs to be. She is funny, smart, and appropriately serious at times. She is a hard worker and intentional with her love. She is beautiful inside and out, and it is clear to me that she is a gift from God because He loved me that much.

My job is to steward her and His love toward her. As with any gift, I should continually be thankful for the Lord's compassion and grace in my life. The best example that I have of His grace is my wife.

Chapter 29

TRANSITION

Reid Lehman, Miracle Hill's thirty-year CEO, decided to retire from the ministry in 2015, and the board went through an extensive search and prayerfully hired a replacement. Reid left and began consulting for other ministries throughout the nation and abroad.

When Reid retired, I was the director of Overcomers and loving my life and career. Soon after, I was promoted to vice president of adult ministries as my longtime mentor and friend, Bill Slocum, similarly retired. I found myself leading all of Miracle Hill's shelters, recovery programs, and transitional housing. Somehow, I found myself in a ministry position that had, in my experience, been filled by a couple of the wisest men I had ever known. I had recently finished my master's in business and in this new role was quickly putting it to work. I also found myself in the middle of the most challenging relational period in Miracle Hill's recent history. Our ministry identity was being challenged, and our future seemed uncertain. For the first time in my ministry experience I was struggling daily, caught in a seemingly never-ending tide of stress.

Over the course of two years, I asked the Lord if it was time to leave, and each time He told me no. Several times, as opportunities became apparent, I tried to twist the Lord's arm, but He clearly showed me in my devotional times and through prayer that I was exactly where He wanted me.

By June of 2017, Reid's replacement was gone, and Reid humbly returned to the ministry in an interim capacity. As Miracle Hill was floundering culturally, relationally, and financially, Reid's first job was to restabilize the ship. People were hurting for many reasons that are not worth getting into, other than to say that Reid sensed appropriately that the board should let him help the ministry heal before they replaced him again. At the time, I do not think anyone knew how difficult and stressful a task this meek man of God took on. Reid's humility, patience, and gentle leadership were reassuring to many of us, but it was easy to see how the pressure to realign the ministry was wearing on him. We had lost significant trust from our donors and friends, and there were hurting people at every level of leadership across the ministry. Over the next year, I had a front row seat watching Reid struggle spiritually, emotionally, and mentally. In retrospect, I can see that when he retired the first time, he removed the mantle of leadership, and upon his return, he had to put the weight of the ministry back on himself during a more challenging time frame. Reid showed us that serving God means doing what He asks you to do, even when it is uncomfortable.

Over the next year, God slowly facilitated healing across the breadth of the ministry, internally, externally, and at every level of leadership. God was guiding us back in the right direction, and everyone involved could feel the shift. We leaders spent time more clearly defining our identity and culture to make it harder to ever shift off course again.

In the spring of 2018, the board began a search for a new CEO. Reid had worked hard with those of us on the senior leadership team to better define our culture, values, and identity as a ministry, and the board was poised to lead with those definitional elements in mind during this new season of leadership transition.

Several leaders, including myself, were invited to meet with the board to explore possible candidacy for the CEO position. I had zero desire to move into the role but respected our board and the process. I frankly took the opportunity to tell them how disinterested I was in the position and to offer my thoughts on how they should go about choosing the next person. All internal candidates told them the same thing.

I had watched the position eat up Reid's replacement for eighteen months. Then I watched it get to Reid upon his return. Reid lost weight and sleep in equal measures for months; the weight of the world was on his shoulders. I certainly felt called to serve, but not to get eaten alive by stress. I reasoned that I had a wife and young children and wanted to continue to keep those people safe and close, and not lose my sanity and health to ministry.

The board hired an outside firm to help with the search, and they began looking far and wide for who the Lord was calling. In the spring of 2019, I was asked to reconsider applying for the position. Nothing had changed for me emotionally or spiritually. I did not feel the Lord calling me to pursue this, nor did I selfishly want the perceived added stress. I had peace in life that I dared not challenge, falsely thinking that my decisions have anything to do with maintaining God's peace. After talking the invitation over with my wife, I remembered a truth that had served me well for many years at this point: God doesn't care what I want to do.

He loves me endlessly. He often asks more of me than I want to give. Everything good I have in my life is because I let the Lord, through His word and His people, direct my decision. Because I didn't listen to myself, I went to the food warehouse, which changed my vocational and spiritual life forever. Because I didn't listen to myself, I have a beautiful wife, two amazing children, and a family that loves me. Because I didn't listen to myself, I am not face down in a gutter, or worse, face up in a box six feet under the ground.

I landed on doing what had worked successfully in life, obedience. I told the wise counsel around me that I would enter the process and see where the Lord led. In my heart, I knew there was nothing to lose, until there was.

Some weeks later, I had an initial interview with the board followed by a round of personality and skills testing facilitated by the search firm. To my surprise, I soon learned that I had been chosen to go to a second round of interviews, which would be with the whole board and then a separate interview with my co-laborers in the vineyard. Because I was a candidate, I would no longer be able to know what the board was discussing or who they were considering; I would not be a part of the internal hiring process moving forward.

Here I went back to the woodshed with Jesus. Up to this point, I had not consciously committed to the pursuit of the position. Lauren and I knew that to move to the next stage, I would have to simultaneously express my desire for the position and trust a process that I could no longer influence.

We perceive emotional freedom from decisions that we act on or believe we do not care about. As long as I was just a pawn on the board, then the outcome did not matter. By expressing my desire for this role publicly and personally, I was exposing myself to vulnerability. Lauren says that I am brutally transparent with people, but extremely guarded in areas of vulnerability. She knows me well enough to understand I am willing to talk about all kinds of uncomfortable things as long as I perceive safety in the openness. The candidacy would require me to open myself up to getting hurt, and I knew it. If I stayed in the process, I couldn't meet, question, or pursue understanding around the candidates.

Lauren also says that I find comfort in what I perceive I can control. Given the history of the past few years at Miracle Hill, losing a voice in the process terrified me. If I can't influence the situation, then I will be stuck with an outcome that I had no say in:

- What if I stayed in the process and they hired somebody who was a bad fit and we went back down the rabbit hole?
- What if I stayed in it, expressed a deep desire to serve in this capacity, and was rejected?

On top of these questions was a laundry list of insecurities bubbling to the surface about who I was and what the reality might be if they picked me.

- What if I am not good enough?
- What if I flounder and the ministry fails?
- What if the stress gets to me and I relapse?
- What if I fail my family?
- What if I am rejected by man?

Lauren and I committed ourselves to prayer, and as I opened myself up to God's leading, I found the peace that only God gives—not at all counterfeit but rather a peace imbedded into every cell of my body. This peace and His word guided my thoughts and laid a machine gun to my insecurities.

> The fear of man lays a snare, but whoever trusts the LORD is safe.
> —Proverbs 29:25

> Whatever you do, work heartily, as for the Lord and not for men.
> —Colossians 3:23

> Now may the God of peace who brought again from the dead our Lord Jesus, the great shepherd of the sheep, by the blood of the eternal covenant, equip you with everything good that you may do his will, working in us that which is pleasing in his sight, through Jesus Christ, to whom be glory forever and ever. Amen.
> —Hebrews 13:20–21

A week or two after the interviews were finished, I got a call from one of Miracle Hill's board members who was the chair of the CEO Search Committee. After exchanging pleasantries, he explained that the board had tasked him with asking me a difficult question: "Ryan, is there anything from your past that could come back to hurt Miracle Hill?"

Well, faithful reader, up to this point you have read a sanitized version of the events of my life. As I stated many pages ago, I have avoided sharing the details as I do not think they benefit anyone to read. After wrestling with the question, I suggested that he and I have a meeting where I could tell him everything, all the gritty details. My reasoning was that by telling the board the whole story in detail, they could never come back to me and say, "We didn't know." I wanted to put the decision in God's hands. All of it.

He agreed and we scheduled a time when the two of us and another board member could meet. The day came and both men came into my office; I could see that they were uncomfortable. It wasn't that they didn't want to have the conversation as they both clearly were prepared to do whatever was necessary to protect the ministry, but I think they didn't want me to have to spill my guts to them. Over the course of an hour, I told them everything. I am sure it was as uncomfortable for them to hear it as it was for me to say it. I had only talked about most of those details one other time in the quiet of a counselor's office.

After the meeting I leaned back in my chair quietly laughing and thought to myself, "*Well, that's the end of that.*" Lauren and I had a good laugh about it that night, and while Lauren was encouraging me to have faith, be patient, and trust, I honestly believed that the horrible things I shared with those two kind and gracious men were the kiss of death for the board's discernment process. I could not reason that anyone would trust the leadership of this ministry to someone like me.

A week later, Jon, Miracle Hill Board member and Search Committee chair, set up another formal meeting with me that I was sure was my *Dear John* meeting, pun intended. It wasn't. The board had unanimously voted to ask me to be Miracle Hill's next CEO. I was floored. A chief of sinners as a chief executive officer. The Lord has an amazing sense of humor. Lauren and I prayed over the weekend, and I accepted the job in the late summer of 2019. I was announced in the fall and moved into the position January 1, 2020.

Wow. What a big God we serve.

I am a broken sinner saved by grace. I offer nothing to the ministry that it cannot get from some other source or person. While Jesus has done a great work in my life, I am a criminal who deserves prison and death . . . **but God**.

God doesn't need us to be anything except willing and obedient. Most leaders either perceive that they are ill-equipped or unprepared, and this feeling isn't something new.

> *And I said: "Woe is me! For I am lost; for I am a man of unclean lips, and I dwell in the midst of a people of unclean lips; for my eyes have seen the King, the* Lord *of hosts!*
> —Isaiah 6:5

Isaiah thought he was unworthy to do the will of the Father, but God had other plans.

> *But Moses said to the* Lord, *"Oh, my Lord, I am not eloquent, either in the past or since you have spoken to your servant, but I am slow of speech and of tongue." Then the* Lord *said to him, "Who has made man's mouth? Who makes him mute, or deaf, or seeing, or blind? Is it not I, the* Lord? *Now therefore go, and I will be with your mouth and teach you what you shall speak." But he said, "Oh, my* Lord, *please send someone else."*
> —Exodus 4:10–13

Moses likewise believed himself to be unequipped and, at the burning bush, he came up with a variety of excuses from his speech to his perception that the people won't listen to him. Again, God had other plans.

And the LORD *turned to him and said, "Go in this might of yours and save Israel from the hand of Midian; do not I send you?" And he said to him, "Please, Lord, how can I save Israel? Behold, my clan is the weakest in Manasseh, and I am the least in my father's house."*
—Judges 6:14–15

Let's not forget Gideon who we are first introduced to when he is in hiding. He also tries to run from the call God has on his life, but God had other plans. In his case, one man and an army of 300 would take on tens of thousands of Midianites.

And the list goes on.

I have no idea what your story is or what army is standing in front of you. I don't know what lies your past is telling you about you. I only know one thing: God is bigger than all those things. He can use you if you will let go. He can direct you if you will listen.

In 2023 my pastor, Travis Agnew, was working through the book of Exodus, and near the end of one of his sermons, he said something that greatly impacted me:

We often pray that God will lead, guide, and direct us. I have learned that this is a faulty way of thinking. God's Word shows us that He will always lead, guide, and direct us. Instead of praying for His leadership, I should pray that I will follow. Instead of praying He will guide me, I should pray I will listen. Instead of praying that He will direct me, I should pray that I will obey.[1]

---

1 Travis Agnew, "God Leads Through Paths Unexpected" (sermon), Rocky Creek Church, April 16, 2023, Greenville, SC.

Wow. If I follow Him and His way, He will lead, guide, and direct me in all that I do. My job then is to be a follower of His leadership, guidance, and direction—His way of living.

This is the way that we, together, can deal with the pressures and challenges we face every day in our lives and in ministry. Jesus never says that life will be easy, but He clearly says that following Him, listening to His leading, and being obedient to His direction is the way we should live. This is the path to peace.

In the Gospel of Luke, Zechariah's prophesy speaks to the path of peace found only in God:

> *Because of the tender mercy of our God, whereby the sunrise shall visit us from on high to give light to those who sit in darkness and in the shadow of death, to guide our feet into the way of peace.*
>
> —Luke 1:78–79

We shouldn't weigh ourselves by our past; Jesus doesn't. Our past is as far from who we are as the east is from the west. If we are obedient, Jesus has a plan for our lives that makes our wildest dreams seem tame. Again, not easy, but if we follow him, we better buckle up.

My favorite quote by the Christian theologian C. S. Lewis comes from his epic and symbolic fantasy series *The Chronicles of Narnia*. In one description of Aslan, the representation of Jesus in the book, Mr. Beaver says to Susan and Lucy:

> "Safe?" said Mr. Beaver . . . "Who said anything about safe? 'Course he isn't safe. But he's good. He's the King, I tell you."[2]

---

2 C. S. Lewis, *The Lion, the Witch and the Wardrobe* (Grand Rapids, MI: ZonderKidz, 2005), 146–147.

It isn't safe to follow Jesus. He might take us somewhere we feel completely unprepared to go. But everything He directs in our lives is the best we can have. It is not easy to follow Jesus. But the path He has us on, no matter how rocky, is where we should be. It can be scary to follow Jesus. But wherever He takes us will be a path of real peace in our lives.

> *Peace I leave with you; my peace I give to you. Not as the world gives do I give to you. Let not your hearts be troubled, neither let them be afraid.*
> —John 14:27

I dare you to trust Him.

Chapter 30

2020

My first official day as president and chief executive officer of Miracle Hill was January 1, 2020. To be honest, other than being in a new office and having to do some extra interviews, not a whole lot was different. The ministry's senior leadership team still met weekly to deal with the realities of operating the Upstate's largest residential ministry for those experiencing homelessness. I started meeting with Reid weekly, daily initially, to learn aspects of the position in which I was grossly uneducated and unprepared. More importantly I drank from the fountain of wisdom that he graciously offered to me. I know I am a blessed man to have had Reid in my life during this transition and to this day.

Miracle Hill's board has six meetings a year with a daylong board retreat in February. This means that from December to early February, the CEO is preparing to have the board monitor his performance for the previous year. That meeting would be Reid's last official meeting with the board. Essentially, the schedule of the retreat is such that in the morning, Reid reported the outcomes from the previous year, and in the afternoon, I helped facilitate discussions about the future. Because I did not know anything about being a CEO and very little about policy governance, Reid helped me to prepare for the meeting. Overall, there were clear skies across the ministry and the meeting went fine. None of us could see what was right over the horizon.

By late February we had begun to hear of a new disease spreading across the world. Some respiratory illness called COVID-19 was spreading very fast and was threatening to get into the US. Some news agencies were reporting spotty cases on the west coast, but nothing that could threaten dear old South Carolina.

By the first week of March, we were seeing it everywhere across the US, including South Carolina, and alarm bells were ringing in the news every day. I know all of you experienced this in your own world and remember how little we knew. No one knew how deadly it was. No one knew how it spread. No one knew how to stop it.

On any given day Miracle Hill has over six hundred people living in one of our residential facilities. A quick moving respiratory illness can mean disaster when most of your populations live in congregate living facilities. We also had our annual fundraising banquet scheduled for mid-March.

As the days went by, the talking heads on the national stage began to talk about staying home unless it was absolutely necessary to go out. Local news agencies parroted this narrative. While we prayed and waited to see what would happen, the news just kept getting more fear-based as the number of cases grew, and the number of deaths reported skyrocketed. Tim Smith, our vice president of human resources, started engaging in nearly daily calls with the CDC from this point and for more than a year. In one call that I was on with national leaders, we were told that the population of those experiencing homelessness would be one of the hardest hit demographics, and that we could expect to see 50 to 100 thousand homeless people die in the first six months.

After talking with anyone who could give me wisdom and guidance on dealing with this difficult situation, I prayerfully made the first major decision as CEO of the ministry and canceled our annual banquet. Trust me, this is the last thing I wanted to do at the time, but we did not have any options that we thought would be safe for our friends, volunteers, staff, and donors. Many of our friends are not young, and the jury was out on the virulence of the pathogen.

I remember talking to Reid and having him encourage me that I should, as much as was reasonably possible, not listen to the world, but listen to the Lord and do what He told me to do. While I agreed with him in theory, for years I had always had someone who could ultimately make the hard decisions. This time the buck stopped with me and Jesus. I had never been more thankful to be surrounded by amazing men and women of God to pray with and seek Jesus with. This banquet typically provides around five to seven percent of our cash donations for the year and it had not been canceled, ever, that anyone could remember.

We had already generated some videos to play at the banquet, and we brainstormed an idea that we would do a virtual banquet. Today all of you know what this is, but in March of 2020, this was truly innovative, and it was the brainchild of Jacob Edmisten and his amazing team of devoted development employees. Monday of that week, Jacob and I traveled all around Miracle Hill and filmed update videos. The team let all the registered banquet attendees know that they could now watch the banquet online virtually. We asked Reid to meet us that afternoon in Pickens at the Children's Home on Miracle Hill, the site for which our ministry was named, to film an intro video. That night, like a mad scientist, Jacob stayed up and put the whole video together. We had a virtual banquet the very next night after finalizing the video and its upload to Facebook and YouTube just hours before we were to press Play. God, as He always does, showed up and showed out. We received nearly the same amount of donations through this virtual banquet as we had budgeted for with the live banquet. Looking forward a year, we had a second virtual banquet that we had months to prepare for. I think the first one was better; the Lord's favor and DNA were all over that chaotic event.

After we escaped what could have been a nightmare for the banquet, the situation went from bad to worse. The masks, gloves, and sanitizer that would color our lives for years came into play, and we leaders found ourselves in a COVID-19 meeting every morning of the week. We had to tell our volunteers to stay home, which represented 50,000 hours of annual work or the equivalent of twenty-five full-time staff members; all those random tasks were absorbed by our staff. The residential staff had to figure out how to operate a facility for social distancing while everyone lived in bunks three feet away from each other—an impossible equation.

One afternoon, I came across an article written about the Christian response during plagues across history; the Lord used that article to season my thinking. In it the author detailed how during plagues over the past two thousand years, when the world ran away from the fire, believers ran into it. When the world shut its doors, Christians opened theirs, and many went to their reward as a result. No matter the disease—smallpox, yellow fever, or the black plague—Christians ran into the fire and served their neighbors. While many shelters and services were shutting their doors across the nation, I felt the Lord strongly leading us to do our job now more than ever. If we shut our doors, then where do the people go? Miracle Hill kept its doors open and accepted new guests every day, 365 days a year, throughout the pandemic.

If we are afflicted, it is for your comfort and salvation; and if we are comforted, it is for your comfort, which you experience when you patiently endure the same sufferings that we suffer. Our hope for you is unshaken, for we know that as you share in our sufferings, you will also share in our comfort.

—2 Corinthians 1:6–7

*Even if I am to be poured out as a drink offering upon the
sacrificial offering of your faith, I am glad and rejoice with
you all.*

—Philippians 2:17

Inevitably, COVID-19 hit Miracle Hill and began to spread into
the population of those experiencing homelessness. Luckily, we were
ready. A month or more earlier, we had started meeting with all the
players in town who could be helpful during this nightmare. We had a
standing meeting every couple of days with the infectious disease leaders
at Prisma Health, the CDC, New Horizon Family Health Services,
DHEC, Bon Secours, and dozens of other community partners. While
South Carolina prepared to create a tiered quarantine shelter system for
positive COVID-19 patients, Miracle Hill became the guinea pig, and
opened the state's first Tier 1 quarantine shelter for COVID-19 positive
patients who had nowhere to go.

After much prayer, I had the most humbling leadership experience
of my life. I explained to the staff what we were doing and told them
that I would not force anyone to work in this shelter filled with infected
people, but I asked them to consider whether the Lord was calling them
to work in this space. Hands went up across the ministry with staff
members saying: *"Here I am Lord, send me."*

Wow. It wasn't just residential staff, but staff from all areas,
experiences, and demographics. Young staff members who didn't have
family at home showed up, and staff who were grandparents and had
everything to lose showed up. They cared each day for the guests we
had in this shelter. One man who came from the hospital had never
heard of us or been to a Miracle Hill facility before. For two full weeks,
he was the only patient in the quarantine shelter. This meant that the
whole spiritual weight of these committed employees was solely devoted
to caring for this man, twenty-four hours a day. How amazing that the
Lord would build a shelter, and for two weeks, shower one person with
more care and attention than seems possible. I am sure that this guy was

tired of hearing about Jesus all day every day by the end of it, but there is no doubt he heard the good news of the gospel.

What do you think? If a man has a hundred sheep, and one of them has gone astray, does he not leave the ninety-nine on the mountains and go in search of the one that went astray?
—Matthew 18:12

As we implemented the quarantine shelter, we began to struggle with our thrift stores, and by default, we struggled financially. Our amazing thrift stores were contributing approximately two million dollars a year back to the ministry in 2019, and one of the first COVID-19 side effects was that a lot of people stopped shopping. Where we typically saw $40,000 a week coming from the stores to support the ministry, that dropped to twenty, then to ten, then to nothing, then quickly into the negatives.

Then the world shut down. One morning I got to my office around six and quickly learned that the governor had ordered all retail stores to shut their doors. What had been a challenging financial crisis, quickly became the sinking of the Titanic.

While the stores were open, we still had nearly enough sales to pay the thrift employees, but the minute they were ordered shut, 150 Miracle Hill employees were sent home, and we still had to figure out how to pay them. As a nonprofit, and one with lower-than-normal turnover, we are a noncontributor to state unemployment. This means that any staff member who goes on unemployment is funded by the ministry rather than the state. No one in their wildest imagination could have dreamed of half the workforce going on unemployment at the same time.

The stress and chaos led me to momentarily believe that the Lord had put me into the CEO role to steward its destruction in the first six months. We were sinking financially at a rate that was unsustainable.

One day Reid and I met privately to discuss all that was happening across the ministry. Prior to the CEO shift, Reid had humbly agreed to be with me through the first eighteen months of transition and to give me all the wisdom he had learned over decades of experience. As I unpacked all the decisions and challenges of the road we were on, Reid sat quietly. Once I was done, he sat back in his chair with a big smile on his face and said, "I promised to share everything I learned in leadership over the years, but I never had a pandemic, so I got nothing for you."

This was Reid's way of lightening the mood, and I believe at the same time he was quietly telling me to trust Jesus, not him. I knew Reid would ride it out with me, and Reid knew the most important thing he could do for me during this season was to pray for me. He told me he did every day, and I believed him. What a friend we have in Jesus and what a friend I have in Reid.

One of the cultural practices at Miracle Hill that I had always appreciated was that whenever we get into a tough situation, we don't carry the burden alone. Reid had always been good about calling "prayer and listening" session where he could invite the staff to meet at a certain time to pray corporately for an issue. Sometimes, the prayer lasts for an hour or two. Once the prayer time is complete, we go around the room and share what we feel like the Lord said or impressed on us during that time. In the past few months, we had already had several of these sessions as we walked through COVID-19, but with the stores closing, we gathered again to hear from the One who has all the answers.

There were about fifty of us sitting in a room together and another fifty on a conference call in the middle of the circle. We spent considerable time in prayer.

> *Do not be anxious about anything, but in everything by prayer and supplication with thanksgiving let your requests be made known to God. And the peace of God, which surpasses all understanding, will guard your hearts and your minds in Christ Jesus.*
>
> —Philippians 4:6–7

Let me pause this story to describe to you how I was feeling and doing. I was miserable. I was barely sleeping and have never been more stressed in my life. Every day we had to react to some new rule coming out of Washington, and we had hundreds of staff members and hundreds of guests counting on us to make wise decisions. On top of that, the world was divided, as it is now, and whatever decision we made as a senior leadership team, fifty percent of our staff, guests, and constituents didn't agree with us. Every decision was a giant point of contention. While I prayed more during this time than I remember praying and seeking in the past, the physical and emotional toll on me was unbelievable.

After we finished praying, we went around the room and without fail, everyone in the room, in one way or another said the same thing: "Do nothing and trust the Lord."

When it was my turn to speak, I do not remember having much to say, as I couldn't get out of my own head long enough to hear the Lord or anyone else for that matter. I sat there quietly weeping and begging God for clarity. After the meeting concluded, Reid met me in the hallway and exclaimed, "Isn't this exciting. The Lord spoke clearly, and we should just wait for him!"

I emotionally responded, "No, it isn't exciting," and walked away. In my brokenness and confusion, I wanted something physical that I could grasp, some decision I could make, some tangible way I could fix the problem, and God was telling me to do nothing. At least He was telling others who were in turn telling me to do nothing.

He has said that to me a lot in life, and I would love to say I am sanctified enough to love that answer, but I don't. God built me to be a fixer, and when He won't hand me a wrench, it feels scary, reminding me of being out of control in my previous life. I pray often that the Lord would help me to be at peace in the waiting. The nothing is always harder for me than the something.

While I did not like the experience or the Lord's answer through His people, I hadn't gotten to this place in life by going my own way. While I didn't like it, I was obedient.

It was April 2020, and we had a development goal of $300 thousand. Over the course of the month, the Lord sent us $900 thousand. We are lost on our own strength . . . but God. The same God who sent a truckload of juice and jelly many years earlier sent a truckload of support when the going got tough.

> But he said to me, "My grace is sufficient for you, for my power is made perfect in weakness." Therefore I will boast all the more gladly of my weaknesses, so that the power of Christ may rest upon me. For the sake of Christ, then, I am content with weaknesses, insults, hardships, persecutions, and calamities. For when I am weak, then I am strong.
> —2 Corinthians 12:9–10

The same thing happened in May, then June, and throughout the rest of the pandemic. God knew that we couldn't do anything, and He didn't need us to. He sent an army of His people to hold us up. The one person I couldn't point to as having anything to do with that miraculous provision was myself.

I learned more in the gauntlet of 2020 than I ever could have learned in ten years of normal ministry operation. I learned to trust Him in a way that I couldn't have without COVID-19. I am not saying that the Lord created COVID-19 for my benefit, but He certainly used it for my good and His glory. I found peace in the storm, but as is often true in life, peace comes after you have walked through the fire, not before it.

Chapter 31

BENJI AND EVELYN

W hen Lauren and I started having children, I idealized what kind of father I wanted to be and how I wanted to raise my children. I knew that I wanted to be present in their lives and not have a career or distraction pull me away from them to the point that they would not miss me when I am gone. Shortly after Lincoln was born, I heard Harry Chapin's famous song *Cat's in the Cradle* with my new set of father's ears. The song talks about busyness and pursuit of career over family. I had no idea that this song was a tragedy rather than a melancholy folk song. In this epic tale, the father is too busy for the son and then when the father is old, his son is just like him and is too busy for him. It is super sad. Stop what you are doing and listen to the song if you have kids.

Anyway, the song and the experiences from my life, have led me down a parenting path where I want to be as involved in my kids' lives as is healthy. I know I am not supposed to be their friend, but I want my kids to know I love them and for them to recognize I want what is best for them in every scenario. I also deeply want to have experiences with my kids that they will never forget.

As is typical, we who parent, end up trying to get our kids to do the things we enjoy doing. I was a soccer player growing up, so naturally, both my kids play soccer, and they still want me to coach them. I was a swimmer growing up, so naturally, both my kids are on a swim team. Go Gators! And on and on it goes . . . as I did, I want my kids to do. I hunt, so they sit in a tree with me in the fall. I love endurance sports, they currently do not agree, but perhaps one day they will.

One of the activities I have found great joy in as an adult is backpacking, and I have slowly been working my kids into a desire to go out in the woods, into God's creation, walk a long way, and then sleep uncomfortably in the woods before walking a long way back out. When Lincoln was four, we slept in a tent in the yard and cooked marshmallows over a fire. I talked up the experience of camping with him for a few years until he was chomping at the bit to go on a "real" camp out. At six I felt like he was ready, and the time finally came for me to plan our first overnight backpacking trip. Because I like things on the extreme, I wanted to make it seem more intense than it was and although it was only going to be at a local state park, I planned a hiking route that was a little over four miles to the campsite. Lincoln and I planned this outing for months, and his excitement was contagious. He asked every week if this was the week we were going.

Eventually, the weekend came, and I loaded us up and drove to the park. Knowing that we only had to hike four miles to camp, which seemed short to me, I packed too much gear and food into my bag, knowing that I wanted Lincoln to have an enjoyable experience. In his brand-new backpack all I put was water and his sleeping bag, reasoning those ten pounds or so was a good introduction to rucking gear for a six-year-old.

So, we set off on the trail, my son having never hiked more than two miles in his life to my knowledge. About an hour in, the pack became too much for him. I took it and threw it on top of my already overloaded pack. Two and a half hours into the hike, we made it to our campsite and set up camp. We were alone on the bank of a pristine mountain lake in a beautiful location. The weather was perfect, and it was everything I had dreamed up in my head. We had a typical camping lunch of flatbread sandwiches, chips, and snack bars. I got out our fishing gear, and we set out to catch a whopper.

About twenty minutes into fishing, black storm clouds started rolling around the lake. I knew ahead of time there was a chance of afternoon showers, as is typical in summer. I looked over at Lincoln to see anxiety and fear in his eyes. He had never been so far away from civilization, and as the clouds rolled in, his desire to be in the middle of nowhere rolled out. I can't recall seeing true fear on his face before this moment, and I instantly wanted to relieve his concern for his circumstances. I watched him for a few minutes and then offered him a choice.

"Son, it looks like we might get some rain."

"Will we be, OK?"

"Yes, we will be fine. It might thunder and lightning for a while, but we will be safe and warm in the tent."

He uneasily retorted, "Are you sure?"

Now I was left with a dilemma. I didn't want to scare my son from wanting to camp ever again, but I also wanted him to face his fear. I finally explained the situation to him and gave him a choice.

"Lincoln, here are your choices, and I am fine with either decision. We can stay; it might get loud and wet for a while, but we will be fine. Or we can leave. We can go home and sleep in our beds tonight, but let me be clear, there is no fast way out. We would have to pack our stuff up and hike a few hours out, and if we are going to go, we have to go now so we are out before dark."

It was obvious in his body language that he didn't want to disappoint me, but I reassured him.

"Buddy, I am perfectly fine if you want to go home, and we can try it again another day."

He looked at the ground, hiding his big fat tears and whispered, "Dad, I want to go home."

I quickly went to work cleaning the camp up and packed up all the extra gear I brought, which at this point didn't seem like a good idea at all.

We set out on the trail, and although my legs were stiff from the hike in, I quickly found my rhythm and locked into a reasonable pace for Lincoln. This time he lasted about forty-five minutes before the pack started lagging him further behind me. I fastened the pack onto mine again raising my load back over fifty pounds.

Luckily, the storm clouds seemed to pass; we didn't get rained on, but we were not out of the woods literally by a long shot. Another hour went by, and I could see Lincoln starting to falter. We were probably more than seven miles in for the day, and his little legs were giving out on him.

We eventually made it to a trailhead, and I knew if we continued on the trail, we had about another mile to go. If I got off the trail and followed the road, I could probably shave a quarter mile, so we diverted. Again, we started walking. I was a man on a mission, but the reality of the day, the distance, and the weight started to build fatigue in my bones.

Five minutes later, I turned around to see Lincoln limping and wincing with each step. He had a look of determination on his face, but he couldn't hide his pain. I stopped there on the side of the road and asked, "Buddy, do you want me to carry you for a while to give your legs a break?"

"No, Dad, you don't have to do that."

"Are you sure, Buddy? It isn't a big deal at all."

"No way, Dad. You are already carrying so much, and it will hurt you."

"No way; I'm fine, Buddy, come here."

I took the hiking poles that we both had, extended his, and made a bench to put under his legs. I picked him up and he laid his head on my shoulder. While this seemed like it was adding struggle, it actually evened the weight I was carrying and relieved some pressure on my back as I now had fifty pounds on both sides of me.

I had no clue how far we were from my car, but understood I had no choice but to keep moving forward.

Over the next thirty minutes, we were passed by car after car. What a sight we must have been; a bearded sweaty man holding a giant backpack and a child. No one stopped to ask if we were OK, however. I thought someone in each car that drove toward us might offer assistance, but they just kept on driving.

As my breathing began to reflect the wear on my body, a four-door jeep drove up and stopped. A guy yelled out the window asking if we could use a ride, and I immediately said we would love a ride.

My new friend Benji immediately pulled over and jumped out of his vehicle. Now before you think I am putting my son in harm's way by hitchhiking, we were in a state park, and I had plenty of "equipment" with which to defend myself. Another way of saying that is that I was armed to defend myself from a bear if necessary. I knew we were only moments from the car.

Benji jumped out, and I got a good look at him. He was older than me and had more gray in his beard. He was covered in tattoos, and had huge, gauged earrings dangling. He ran over to the bed of his late model Jeep Gladiator and popped open the tailgate. I put Lincoln down and put my pack into his truck bed. My shoulders and lower back screamed with relief. I offered for us to sit in the bed of the vehicle because we were filthy, sweaty, and smelled terrible, but he wouldn't hear it. He cranked up his AC, cleared off his backseat, and insisted that we get comfortable in the vehicle. I gratefully accepted his offer and slid into his vehicle, which smelled of pungent marijuana smoke. This is where I met Evelyn who instantly smiled, asked our names, and offered us a cold soda. Benji did a three-point turn and headed out to find our vehicle and asked me a simple question: "Hey, Ryan, it is not a problem at all to assist. We would do this for anyone because of our friend Jesus. Do you know Him?"

Yes, you read that correctly. Benji began to evangelize me. We had a great conversation, prayed together once we got to the vehicle, and he gave Lincoln a bracelet that said, "God loves you."

Now I am not a betting man normally, but of the four of five vehicles that passed me walking on the side of the road, I think it is fair to assume that at least half of them go to some type of church. We were in a state park in the Deep South. Yet no one stopped except Benji. I was clearly in distress, and for one reason or another, people just kept driving by.

Benji on the other hand, did not look like he went to church. He was covered in war paint from the world and piercings, and his vehicle smelled of cannabis. He and Evelyn clearly didn't look like they went to church. Do you know who they looked like? They looked like Jesus.

Their lives at first glance do not reflect the perceived holiness we look for from a position of having the moral high ground, but their lives clearly reflected and demonstrated the love of Christ.

You are the light of the world. A city set on a hill cannot be hidden. Nor do people light a lamp and put it under a basket, but on a stand, and it gives light to all in the house. In the same way, let your light shine before others, so that they may see your good works and give glory to your Father who is in heaven.

—Matthew 5:14–16

When I grow up, I want to be Benji, and I want my son to be him too. In my walk with the Lord, He is showing me more and more that our actions speak a lot louder than our words. We can look a certain way, and speak eloquent while practicing Christianese, and our hearts can be so far away from Jesus that He doesn't know us.

"Not everyone who says to me, 'Lord, Lord,' will enter the kingdom of heaven, but the one who does the will of my Father who is in heaven. On that day many will say to me, 'Lord, Lord, did we not prophesy in your name, and cast out demons in your name, and do many mighty works in your name?' And then will I declare to them, 'I never knew you; depart from me, you workers of lawlessness.'"

—Matthew 7:21–23

Benji is a living example of the parable of the Good Samaritan. Benji stopped what he was doing to care for another human being, not because that human being offered him anything in return, but because Benji consciously or unconsciously believed my son and I were valued and loved by God, and that God had put us in his path to demonstrate Christ's love. The good news is, that I already know Jesus. In fact, I recognized the savior in Benji. If I didn't already know Christ, I probably would have heard the truth in the gospel much more clearly through Benji's actions than a thousand sermons.

> *But a Samaritan, as he journeyed, came to where he was, and when he saw him, he had compassion. He went to him and bound up his wounds, pouring on oil and wine. Then he set him on his own animal and brought him to an inn and took care of him. And the next day he took out two denarii and gave them to the innkeeper, saying, 'Take care of him, and whatever more you spend, I will repay you when I come back.' "Which of these three, do you think, proved to be a neighbor to the man who fell among the robbers?" He said, "The one who showed him mercy." And Jesus said to him, "You go, and do likewise."*
> —Luke 10:33–37

You don't have to work at a rescue mission, a church, or be on the mission field to display Christ's love to the world. Every interaction you have is an opportunity to "be" Jesus to the person in front of you. We just have to get over our deeply held fears of rejection and walk in love. We have to recognize our neighbor doesn't have to look like us, come from the same part of town, have the same life experience, or believe what we believe. Our neighbor is anyone, because everyone is made in the image of God. Everyone is knitted together by the Creator and worthy of our love and attention.

The more we recognize these truths, the more Jesus will be real to us and others. If we believe what we say we believe, how are we not doing it all day every day, screaming Jesus from the rooftops? Why are you and I not living out sacrificial love like the ambassadors that God says we are?

I was challenged by Benji and Evelyn's testimony of faith. I need to get out of the boat more often, trust Jesus, and see where He takes me. We should all want to boldly proclaim the truth of the gospel to a broken world, and as the world grows increasingly hostile to the gospel message, it will be our love and compassion lived out, that will pull people in to smell the sweet fragrance of God. Benji embodied true peace and contentment to me and my son, and for that I will be forever humbled and grateful.

Benji, whoever you are and wherever you are, I love you and thank you. Thank you for stepping out of the boat and for keeping your eyes on Jesus.

Chapter 32

JAMES

My wife all but refuses to go out on dates with me in downtown
Greenville. Every time we go, I wind up engaging with every
needy person, panhandler, or homeless person I encounter.
Either I personally know them, or they make the beautiful mistake of
approaching me for conversation. We spend all of our evening serving
rather than enjoying each other's company. She is down for ministry,
but rightfully so, wants each event in its right time. I love the accidental
interactions of the street. When they happen, I see it as a God-directed
relational collision that was ordained for ministry opportunity. In those
moments, in God's will, He chooses you or me to be Jesus to the person
in front of us.

The situation several years ago that caused my wife to establish her
dating directive was a typical Friday night outing for dinner, coffee, and
people watching—our favorite combination. We walked downtown,
through the crowds of an active spring evening, and had just sat down
to dinner at Trios, a unique brick oven pizza restaurant right on main
street. The hostess sat us by the front window as all the outdoor seating
was taken, and that is when I saw James.

James was not someone that I knew personally; he was a face I recognized from the parade of chronically homeless individuals who are planted on or around Main Street. This gentleman is probably in his fifties although he looks like he is in his seventies. He is physically disabled and uses forearm crutches to get around. That evening, he was dirty; he was wearing coke bottle glasses and at least two weeks of unmanaged salt and pepper stubble on his face; his long hair was greasy and unkempt. When I spotted him, James was lying on the ground in the middle of the sidewalk. He was floundering around like a fish out of water at an intersection and appeared to not be able to get back up.

I sat there trying to focus on my menu as I watched dozens of people walk around him on the sidewalk. Each was working desperately to shield their dogs and children from coming close to the pariah who was blocking their path. Their eyes were focused everywhere but at James, although it was clear they saw him. They behaved was as though he was truly invisible to them, but their alert unconscious senses told them some monster lurked where he lay. James, however, was a human being in need. He didn't look like them or behave like them. To be fair to those who passed by, they almost certainly didn't know what to do to help. This creates fear. Fear makes it easy to dismiss a problem as someone else's issue. To quote the ageless sage Yoda: "Fear is the path to the dark side. Fear leads to anger. Anger leads to hate. Hate leads to suffering."

Fear helps us to rationalize our human tendencies as fair, equitable, and righteous. Fear leads us to become angry at someone else's distress as it inconveniences our busy lives: "How dare this hurting human being in front of me stop me from getting to my next appointment. I hate that the city can't control **these** people. Why aren't my tax dollars getting rid of this thing in my path?"

All the while, James, a human being made in God's image, lay helplessly in front of us. I promise you James doesn't want to be there anymore than you want him to be there.

For God has not given us a spirit of fear, but of power, and of love, and of a sound mind.

—2 Timothy 1:7 NKJV

I was not afraid, and I couldn't take it anymore. I excused myself from the table, and my wife just looked at me and smiled. She had seen him as well and knew where I was going. Her smile told me that she knew this human being, knitted together by our mutual Creator, was way more important than my delicious pizza cooking in the oven.

I walked outside toward James and got down on the ground beside him. He was either drunk or had been drinking that day. I could smell the alcohol as it was sweating out of his pores. I asked him if I could help him up and he agreed, not making eye contact with me. I grabbed him by the arms and hoisted him onto the bench directly behind him and we both sat down.

The question I get asked more than any other from a ministry perspective is, "What am I supposed to do when I see someone in need on the street?"

I wish there was a black and white answer that I could give, but in relationship there is no black and white. Everything is bathed in graceful gray in God's economy. The shortest answer I can give, and the one I teach to groups and churches all the time is this: "Fill the need, not the greed."

When someone approaches you on the street with a request or a crudely made sign with their appeal written on it, they are telling you what they want. Most of the time, this request is for food, money, or work. Now here me clearly, I almost never give money, for any reason. There are a few exceptions to this that are directed by God that I will get into shortly, but as a general rule, I do not give money. If the request is for money, I ask what the money is for, and as long as it is a healthy request like food or diapers, I try to fill the need in the context of intentional relationship. We shouldn't do this to alleviate guilt from our own soul, but rather as an olive branch of connection.

A typical interaction goes something like this.

"Hey man, can I get two dollars to get something to eat?"

"I am happy to get you something to eat. There is a Wendy's a block away. Why don't we walk over there, and I will get you whatever you want."

"No, you don't have to do that, just two dollars would be fine."

"Well, I don't carry cash and I don't hand out money, but I am happy to buy you some food, and we can sit down and talk. I'm Ryan, what's your name?"

From there, the conversation takes one of several directions. In some scenarios, the person reverses course and walks away, telling me that they don't like the food I am offering, or they present some other excuse as to why they cannot take me up on the proposition. When this happens, I infer that their need was not great, or their motive was impure.

Sometimes, the person gets angry and calls me names, putting their emotionally or chemically induced frustration on display for all to see. As you can imagine, they were most likely not after food.

Sometimes, the person is like a wounded animal, unsure of my motives. With a lifetime of trauma in their rearview, this often can break relationship before it starts. Their motive might be pure, but the friction they have experienced with the world might be too much to overcome. In these scenarios, I do my best to earn their trust so they will relationally engage. Sometimes, I am successful and sometimes, they walk away due to their own fear.

Sometimes, mental health issues might prevent a willingness to engage. But sometimes, on those glorious, rare occasions, they agree. We walk together to get a supersized meal and wind up having a supersized exchange. The goal is simply to know someone.

Jesus did this. He went out of his way to know people, to engage with them, to get down in the muck with them.

> *They said to him, "Teacher, this woman has been caught in the act of adultery. Now in the Law, Moses commanded us to stone such women. So what do you say?" This they said to test him, that they might have some charge to bring against him. Jesus bent down and wrote with his finger on the ground. And as they continued to ask him, he stood up and said to them, "Let him who is without sin among you be the first to throw a stone at her." And once more he bent down and wrote on the ground. But when they heard it, they went away one by one, beginning with the older ones, and Jesus was left alone with the woman standing before him. Jesus stood up and said to her, "Woman, where are they? Has no one condemned you?" She said, "No one, Lord." And Jesus said, "Neither do I condemn you; go, and from now on sin no more."*
>
> —John 8:4–11

I introduced myself to James and sat down on the bench beside him. We began a conversation in which I tried to discern his needs, and he simply asked for a shake from the fancy ice cream store about a block away. I helped him up, turned to see if I could catch a glimpse of my wife before strolling off in the direction of a shake and a conversation.

I returned to my wife about thirty minutes later and she sweetly told me that they were keeping my food warm in the back. We finished our last weekend date downtown and headed home.

I have no idea what happened to James. I haven't seen him since and to my knowledge he has not checked into the mission, even though I offered to help him get there. I even offered to make some phone calls to get a bed reserved for him. Unfortunately, James was not ready to do something different.

What did we talk about? Life. What flavor of shakes we like. Jesus. How busy it was downtown that evening. We talked like I would talk to anyone else. In this moment, the only skill that I needed was recognizing the equality of humanity. James and I each put our pants on the same way. James and I both know what it is like to want to drink a shake. He and I are both stuck here on this planet trying to figure out our place in the world. Both of us yearn to know the answer to the question, "What does the God of my understanding want from me?" I talked to him like I would talk to you.

Although years have passed, he could still be wandering around Main Street, looking for something evading him in life. Perhaps he is mentally ill. Perhaps an addiction continues to ravage his senses, driving him deeper into madness. Hopefully, he found what he was looking for in life and is doing something different with his time. Sadly, there is a greater chance that he has met his maker. A person cannot exist endlessly in that shape without something giving way, one way or the other.

My life is richer for having shared a shake and a smile with him one spring evening. The only thing that I do differently than most of humanity is see the people God has placed in my path. You can too. These opportunities are all around us if we look for them. They are simply moments God has laid in our path to interact with people He loves just as much as He loves you.

Miracle Hill's philosophy of ministry is built on this idea of intentional relationship. Reid first introduced Miracle Hill to the ideas of nontoxic charity after reading Robert Lupton's book *Toxic Charity*[1] over a decade ago, but the principles established in his book have been the lifeblood of the ministry for eons. We serve those in need to know them, value them, tell them about Jesus, and be Jesus to them when no one else will. For many years there was a sign on the front of our

---

1 Robert D Upton, *Toxic Charity: How Churches and Charities Hurt Those They Help (And How to Reverse It)* (New York: Harper Collins, 2012).

Greenville Rescue Mission that read: "If you can't find a friend in the world, you can find one here."

This is who we are and what we want to do: be a friend to the friendless and family to the orphan. We want people to feel that they are loved by us and by their Creator. The stories Reid shared in *God Wears His Own Watch* serve as a testimony to eighty-plus years of relationship building for Jesus.

Today, our programing exists on the axis of the meeting point of truth and grace. Essentially, this tiered system says to the guest checking into one of our facilities, "The deeper you are willing to go in a relationship with us, the deeper we will go with you."

We open up our Severe Weather Shelters anytime the weather turns cold, dangerous, or deadly. We do this from a position of life and safety knowing that if someone doesn't come in, they may not make it through the night. There is essentially one rule for admittance: They can't be violent to themselves or others. They can enter drunk or high or deranged, and we will offer them food and shelter with compassion, a warm place to sleep, and a shower if they want one. One of our chaplains will probably try to relationally engage with them and tell them about Jesus if they have the ears to hear. Since our Severe Weather Shelter exists in a mostly relational void, we have no expectations for them, and they have to leave the next day.

If that same person chooses to walk around to the front of the building and ask about getting a "regular" shelter bed, but they really do not want much assistance from us, we will check them in to our Crisis Shelter Program. They will understand upon entry that they have to stay sober while they are in the building and attend a few classes. If they do this, they will have a guaranteed bed for thirty days while they get their life in order.

The same person can check in and express to us that they need and desire help. This is where the relational magic happens. Those individuals will make their way into the New Life Program where they agree to the same parameters as the Crisis Shelter participant, but additionally agree to meet with a counselor once a week to develop goals. While we historically have said this is a ninety-day process, life change can take dramatically longer depending on each person's unique circumstances and story. As long as the person is relationally invested in us, we remain committed and relationally invested in them.

OUR PHILOSOPHY

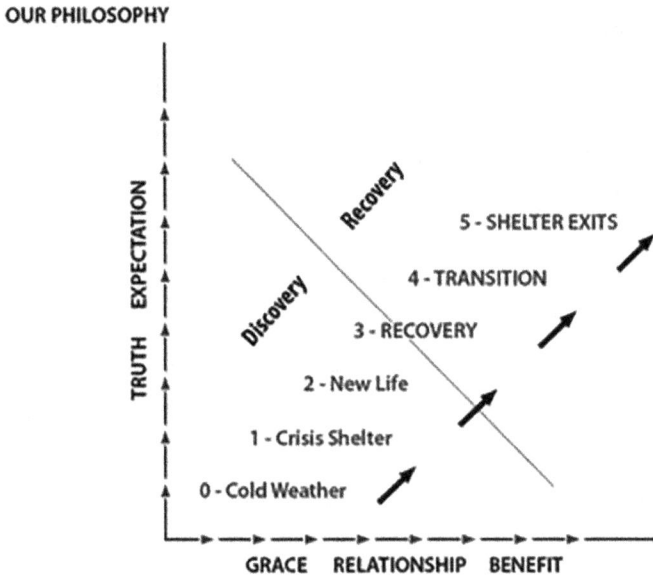

Tier 3 on the diagram is our Christ-Centered discipleship program focused on helping men and women with life-dominating issues and addictions. These guests agree at intake to a seven-month minimal commitment. They additionally agree to attend classes while they forgo employment in lieu of life change.

The summary of the diagram is that the deeper someone is willing to go in relationship with us, the deeper we are willing to go with them. The more they desire grace, and the benefits of residential service, the more relationship we will pour into their lives with higher expectations and increased exposure to truth.

Do you have to be a Christian to stay at Miracle Hill? No. I tell people all the time that you don't have to be a Christian to be here, but you are just going to hear a lot about Jesus if you do. Our deepest desire is that they would see Jesus in the staff, hear the truth of the gospel, and choose to meet Jesus, as I did, in the halls of a Miracle Hill facility.

The amazing staff God has provided at Miracle Hill work diligently to come alongside the guests, advocating and working on their behalf to engage the broken and confusing systems they must deal with each day. Our foster team sheds tears with families who are struggling through the licensing and placements of hurting and lost children. Our thrift stores pray for people's needs who thought they were coming in to buy a pair of pants. We build relationships and sit with people in their grief and brokenness. We work to embrace them in the love of the Father, trusting Him for their needs and healing.

We try to live out our logo in all we do, and offer those who want it, a hand up rather than a handout. Sometimes, when I meet a guy like James on the street, the handout, given relationally, will build enough trust to get him into the front door. Sometimes, it takes years of relationship-building to convince someone that we won't bite, and we want the best for them. Sometimes, a person comes back time and time again, and each time we meet them at the door like it is the first time, smiling and offering friendship and an opportunity to do something different.

"But when he came to himself, he said, 'How many of my father's hired servants have more than enough bread, but I perish here with hunger! I will arise and go to my father, and I will say to him, "Father, I have sinned against heaven and before you. I am no longer worthy to be called your son. Treat me as one of your hired servants."' And he arose and came to his father. But while he was still a long way off, his father saw him and felt compassion, and ran and embraced him and kissed him.

—Luke 15:17–20

We never know when the Lord is going to do a work in someone's life. James might walk into the front door of one of the missions tomorrow. He might be ready to do something different. James could, however, still be on the street. Maybe he is the guy you passed on the sidewalk yesterday, or maybe you will come upon him tomorrow. What will you do differently the next time you are face to face with him? Will you see him, or will you keep on walking.

Chapter 33

FRANKLIN

If you move around the Upstate of South Carolina for a while, you will interact with a whole host of populations, communities, and areas of differing socioeconomic status. We have urban centers, suburbia, rural landscapes, farming, and industrialized areas—all of which you would expect of a growing community in the Deep South. Due to the growth in the area, many previously clearly defined areas are bleeding over into each other. This creates friction at times as populations collide with one another. There is an increased irony of growth as economic prosperity in one community simultaneously exists with redevelopment causing collapse in other communities. The unpopular word here is *gentrification*. If you are here in the Upstate long enough, you might think that you "know" the area—that you know where you should go and where you shouldn't. I am here to say, that if you have never stood in one of Miracle Hill's cold weather shelters on a cold night in January, then you haven't seen the real Upstate. Unlike some other parts of the country, we are really good at hiding our sore spots.

When the weather turns cold or brutal, Miracle Hill opens its shelters to those who have the deepest need. At the beginning of the cold weather season, our census increases by about a hundred people a night across the counties we serve, but if the weather stays cold and the days do not warm, the numbers in these shelters start to rise.

Initially, those who come in are men and women who would typically be living in the shelter but who are not in a shelter for one reason or another. As the season drags on and homelessness on the streets or in the woods gets more difficult, our most challenged friends start to come in from the cold. If we hit a cold snap that lasts for a week or two, people that we don't usually see begin to come out of the woodwork. These individuals do not want to be in the shelter at all, but they make the choice to come in for survival.

These are the most critically ill and antisocial people in our society, and the last thing they want is to be in a big room with a bunch of people talking to them, asking them how they are.

In 2022, I asked Miracle Hill's board to consider coming with me and serving a night in one of our cold weather shelters. Many of them had never seen our shelters operate in this capacity, and those who had knew that this would be an impactful experience. These authentic and devoted warriors of the faith who serve on Miracle Hill's board are always open to a challenge, and they jumped at the opportunity.

Several months later the night came, and I got to the shelter early to greet the board members as they arrived. The staff and guests who work the cold weather shelter set up the room as usual, making sure the mats were out and that blankets and towels were clean. The kitchen prepared a giant pot of chicken noodle soup donated from Whole Foods, and we waited for this evening's guests to begin milling around the rear parking lot of the Greenville Rescue Mission.

One by one guests started to arrive, and it was obvious that while they were walking in from all directions, most of them knew each other. As you might expect, some appeared to be dirty, malnourished, and inebriated. Others arrived by bus or car wearing their work uniforms—usually from a manufacturing plant or fast-food restaurant. As I have said before, homelessness and poverty do not discriminate. These men were young and old, black, and white, all levels of education, and each came with their own story of brokenness. As they piled onto the back deck, smoking, laughing, and clinging tightly to their meager belongings, the scent of body odor, alcohol, and tobacco began to build even in the open-air setting of the back patio.

The board members began pulling in about thirty minutes before we were set to open the shelter, and I walked out to their cars knowing they might feel uncomfortable making their way through the growing crowd. Almost every board member was serving at a cold weather shelter across the ministry that night, some were accompanied by their spouse.

We went inside and the staff assigned each board member to a different task. Two to serve the meal, ladling the hot soup into Styrofoam bowls. Someone to hand out towels. Someone to offer soap, or shampoo, or a washcloth. Each servant went to their station, not knowing exactly what the night and experience would hold for them.

Although I have worked for Miracle Hill for a long time, there is no way to know everyone who chooses to partake in services across the ministry. With over 600 people in care each night, that would be impossible, especially considering the revolving door of those seeking services across the spectrum of service providers in the Upstate. I was wearing a Miracle Hill name tag as did most of the staff and board, but most of the guests had no clue who we were. There is no good reason they would or should care; they are used to seeing sacrificial love through our staff and volunteers. To them, we were just another crew of workers there to serve soup for the night.

I did know a few of the men from my journeys across the ministry, and I quickly fell into conversation with them standing in the cold and dark of the back deck. The dialogue was intermittently broken by a need to quiet a growing argument of someone who was drunk or helping someone in a wheelchair.

Eventually, the time came to open the door and let everyone in one by one. Felicia, one of our newer board members, had been assigned to take everyone's name and birthday as they entered and record it on a sheet. The only form of identification many of these men have is what they are able to articulate or remember. On the surface, this seems like an easy job, but it is not. These men come from so many different walks of life, levels of inebriation, and states of coherency, that understanding what they are saying is probably reasonable about fifty percent of the time. Many times, you have to ask them to repeat themselves, instantly embarrassing everyone involved. Felicia went about her job showing value to each person by saying hello while making eye contact and offering a compassionate smile to each guest.

The night wore on, and the assembly line of service was now in full swing as food was being served. Men were in the bathroom taking showers. Others were already lying down on their mats to get as much warm sleep as possible. All the while the unique experience of the cold weather shelter grew for all of us, some for the first time. As people piled into the gymnasium, the stench grew. I am not saying this in a derogatory way, but the smell of over 100 men, most of whom haven't showered or changed their clothes in weeks is unique; it brings its own character into the room. The noise grows person by person until it becomes a cacophony of curse words and lies; psychosis and whimpers drown out your thoughts until you are just part of the experience in front of you.

As the auditory and olfactory volume grows in the room, so do the opportunities for ministry. As I looked around me, I saw one board member after another engaged in deep conversation with those they were serving. They were offering kindness and attempting to answer questions for which they probably didn't know the answer. Some were just listening, which is often the most potent medicine of ministry.

Several hours into the night, a friend that I will call Franklin entered the room. Franklin is a seventy-three-year-old African American of small stature who uses a cane. I have known him for years, and he is unmistakable for the gray matted dreadlocks on his head and in his beard. The last time I had seen Franklin, he was making progress as a resident of the shelter. He had been navigating his housing needs and waiting for a bed in an affordable living facility for seniors with disabilities. Yet here he was walking in the back door. I do not know why he left the shelter or why he was coming back to a cold weather shelter, but I believe deeply that it is a failure of our society that a senior with a disability doesn't have anywhere better to go. For sure, he is the author of his own decisions, and I am sure his behavior has something to do with his reality. Nevertheless, it hurts my heart to see the elderly with so few options.

Franklin and I locked eyes, and we both beamed with smiles as we approached each other.

"What are you doing here Franklin? You were doing so good!"

"Mr. Ryan, I was going to come by your office tomorrow to talk to you about some things."

"Oh yeah. Well, here I am. What do you want to talk about?"

"Well, there are some things that I think you should know about some of the other men here."

"Brother, I am happy to talk to you about whatever, but what happened? Can we help you get back into the shelter?"

"Mr. Jeremy won't talk to me."

"Well, Franklin it's your lucky day. Jeremy is here right now; let's get him over here and see what we can do about getting you back into the shelter."

Over the next few minutes, Jeremy Huff and I tried to convince Franklin to come up front in the morning to see about checking into a regular bed. We talked with him and prayed with him hoping that he would take us up on the offer. He didn't show over the next few days, but Jeremy and I ran into him a few months later when we were doing a training session at Grace Church—Downtown Campus. As we sat there talking to the pastors and staff about the best way to help those experiencing homelessness, Franklin came into the church to get a coat, and we had an opportunity again to tell him we loved him and ask him to come in out of the cold. He hasn't shown up since then to my knowledge, but I am prayerful that the next time, we will be able to help him find stability.

Toward the end of the night at the cold weather shelter as the men started to settle down and it began to get quiet, Felicia was still at her post, helping the stragglers to sign in and get their mat assignments. A man came in the front door and approached her as he kept looking down to the floor. She asked him his name, and his response stopped her in her tracks.

"Can you say that again, sir?"
He gave his name again.
"Sir, was your mother's name ___?"
"Yes, it was."
"You may not remember me, but my mother and your mother were best friends forty years ago, and you and I used to play when we were children. Do you remember?"
He did.

They spent a few minutes in conversation and after they were done, Felicia came and let some of us know what had just happened. She was clearly shaken by the exchange and had seen the raw brutality of time across a broken world in a way that she couldn't have without that experience.

Felicia and this gentleman had started in similar circumstances, and all these years later, they both were a product of their circumstances and the choices they had made along the way. The experience of homelessness became real in a new way for her because the man was someone she knew; someone she had laughed with as a child.

All the men and women staying in a shelter tonight are someone that someone knows. What they need is for us to know them, to see them.

I think that all the board members who joined us to serve that evening went away with a fresh perspective on what Miracle Hill does, and whom it serves. Perhaps, for some of those guests, the only interaction we will ever have with them is in this capacity. And, therefore, this is our only shot to show them the love of Christ. There was not a great outcome to be documented on a board report—no statistic to brag about; this is a costly venture in which the only currency is the reciprocal love between individuals.

These friends of mine are the realest version of the Upstate you will ever see. These are the people too often forgotten by society; they represent the outcome of sin and brokenness on our generation. While the cast of characters you will see changes each evening, there is one person who is always there, Jesus.

If Jesus, were here in the flesh, where do you think He would be?

Do you think he would be sitting in the front row of your church pew this Sunday?

Would he be in the CEO's office or playing golf with the mayor?

I think he would be sitting with Franklin on a mat in a smelly gym, being a salve for the wounds of his soul and his flesh.

> *Bless the LORD, O my soul, and all that is within me, bless His holy name!*
> *Bless the LORD, O my soul, and forget not all His benefits,*
> *who forgives all your iniquity, who heals all your diseases,*
> *who redeems your life from the pit, who crowns you with steadfast love and mercy,*
> *who satisfies you with good so that your youth is renewed like the eagle's.*
> *The LORD works righteousness and justice for all who are oppressed.*
>
> —Psalm 103:1–6

Some time ago, I was interviewing candidates for our chief operating officer role as my good friend Ken Kruithof was retiring. Our current COO, Justin Boles, who was a candidate at the time, said something profound in his interview. He challenged us with this thought: "We should stop saying we are in the homelessness business and start saying we are in the wholeness business." The point of our identity is not found in the brokenness of our sin and debt, but rather in the wholeness God wants to create in our lives.

This is true for everyone who chooses to trust in Christ and is evidenced by Psalm 103. We are so unworthy, and God is so worthy of our praise. To cement those thoughts, David points to the realities of God, which he is bold enough to call benefits. Forgiveness, healing, redemption, satisfaction are at the top of David's list. He then he points to the fact that God works righteousness and justice for all who are oppressed.

How does Jesus do this? He gets down on a mat and intimately connects with the person in front of Him. He is calling all of us who know Him to do the same. What would the world look like if every cold weather shelter in the nation was flooded with the church every night? What if we all showed up, not because we have anything to offer to another, but because we know Jesus and want to be like Him?

Chapter 34

DMV

E arly in 2023 I realized that I would need to renew my driver's license with DMV when my birthday came around in March that year. This is something we must do every five years. I noted this in my conscious mind and then promptly forgot about it. I remembered again the week of my birthday and began scrambling to get the renewal form together along with the other documents I needed to upgrade to the RealID. I had been putting off this inconvenience for a few years as TSA kept kicking the ball down the field.

The week after my birthday, I took a morning off, went into the DMV and took care of the renewal. I accomplished the RealID upgrade and went to work. That Saturday I received a letter in the mail from the South Carolina DMV notifying me that my license would be officially suspended in the middle of May because of an "issue" originating from the North Carolina DMV.

I have not lived in North Carolina for over twenty years and have not spent any time there outside of the occasional Panthers game with my brother Chris. Since you are a faithful reader, and have made it to this chapter, you recognize that I was a completely different person when I called Charlotte home. I had no clue what the issue could be, and

I immediately started thinking through all the crimes and bad things I was involved with when I did live there. A sense of foreboding and doom colored the weekend for my wife and me. Poor Lauren never knew the delinquent version of me and has never had to deal with the court system or jails, so this was new to her. She did, however, know what she signed up for in our marriage and simply tried to assuage my fears and insecurities. Unfortunately, this was the weekend, and I had to wait until Monday to learn what dumb thing from my past was causing me issues so many years later.

My wife and I had a very interesting conversation over the following few days and decided that God would not have us be fearful about the unknown. We should trust in Him for the outcome as we do everything else in our lives.

Monday came, and Lauren and I got to work on the phones. Eventually, I was able to discern through a handful of phone calls that the issues stemmed from a 1999 Driving Under the Influence charge. Yes, you read that right. A criminal charge from a quarter of a century ago.

During my time at Overcomers in 2003, I remember sitting in a counselor's office and looking at the mountain of issues in front of me. Honestly, I thought that I had dealt with them all. The last set of charges in South Carolina required me to finish out a probation sentence, pay a lot of fees, and take part in South Carolina's Alcohol Dependence and Substance Abuse Treatment Program (ADSAP). That arrest included a violation of probation charge from North Carolina. I completed all the requirements, and South Carolina reinstated my license, which had been suspended from North Carolina. I assumed at the time that my issues with North Carolina were also resolved. Turns out, they were not, and the application for the RealID caused both states to communicate, resurrecting the skeleton in my closet.

My wife and I went into overdrive to resolve the issue. After further phone calls and research, I determined I had to pay a court fee, pay a

DMV fee, and submit to North Carolina's assessment for addiction process. While I worked the next day, Lauren spent time on the phones and found that if I paid the court fee in the mail, as online was not an option, there would be a four-week lag time before the matter could be considered resolved. The courts claimed that their system would need "processing" time. No problem. I jumped in the truck the next day and was in Charlotte within ninety minutes.

The last time I had been in this courthouse, I had been in an orange jumpsuit and shackles. As ridiculous as this was, I experienced a fair amount of anxiety walking through the ornate courthouse doors. I reminded myself who I am in Christ, trusted the Lord, and was back out in my truck in about thirty minutes. I had a little less money in my bank account, but I had knocked out step one of three.

The next few days I spent figuring out how to pay the DMV fee. The process was complicated and confusing, but between my wife and me, we figured it out after a series of phone calls. I paid this fee online, and step two was accomplished.

The third requirement was the drug and alcohol assessment, which I found amusing. Twenty-four years later, North Carolina still wanted its pound of flesh, and there was not a person or judge I could talk to and explain my situation. I made some calls to local organizations to see if I could do the assessment locally and have it approved in North Carolina but found that this would further complicate the situation.

Google helped me find a North Carolina evaluator who would do the assessments virtually. I reached out via email and quickly set up a meeting with her for a few days later. The meeting came, and I took the opportunity to recount all the Lord had done in my life over the years.

- I was saved by the grace of God.
- I was sixteen years sober.
- I was educated, credentialed as a Christian counselor, and ordained as a minister of the gospel.

- I had taught thousands of hours of addiction classes and helped hundreds of men to overcome their addictions.
- I was the chief executive officer of a ministry that helps thousands overcome obstacles in their lives from the experience of homelessness and their own poor decision-making.
- I was emotionally secure, financially stable, and in a healthy marriage.

What did North Carolina think about all these things? Not a whole lot. At the end of the conversation, the evaluator informed me that I would need to complete twenty hours of addiction classes that her firm offered to have the hold on my license released. The Lord had been preparing me for this outcome in my quiet times, and I simply smiled and said, "OK."

Before we hung up, she asked me again if I had completed Overcomers after this arrest, and I said yes. She asked if I could get a letter from the program stating this, and I said, "Well, I usually write those letters, but I can ask the current director of the program if he is willing to write one for me." She told me if I could get a letter, then perhaps she could give me credit for the classes. I had a comical call with Brad Holland, our current Overcomer director when I had to ask him to write letter for me on Miracle Hill letterhead. A few days later, the evaluator received the letter in her inbox, and a few days after that, I got a clearance letter from both the South Carolina and North Carolina DMVs. The issue was resolved.

There are two reasons I am finishing with this personal story in this memoir. The first is to share with you that I had every conceivable advantage in this situation. I have financial means, transportation, education, flexibility in my job, healthy supporting relationships, a sober mind, but still it took my wife and me two weeks to deal with the issue. I had a truck that I could drive to Charlotte and money in my bank account to pay the fee. I had an amazing advocate in my wife, who spent countless hours on the phone on my behalf. I had a computer that allowed me to do things online and have a digital meeting. I had enough flexibility in my job that I could take time out of the day to accomplish these personal goals.

None of Miracle Hill's guests or our neighbors in poverty have most of these advantages. Had this been me twenty years ago, I would have been lost in the chaos of the system, and it would have taken me months to find a way out of the mess, if ever. I remember climbing out of the ditch I had created for myself in my addiction, and it was a deep ditch which took me a long time to climb out. Without a license today, I would have been forced to utilize public transportation, or worse yet, drive illegally on a suspended license to put food in my children's mouth, or take them to school. The system our guests are trying to navigate is not built for their success, but their failure. I am not saying that it is created that way on purpose, but it is a reality faced by our neighbors each day.

During COVID-19, when the schools shut down, what was the single parent supposed to do with their young children while they worked? If an underprivileged family's only car breaks down and they do not have money in the bank to deal with the issue, what are they supposed to do? They can sell their belongings or go to the predatory title loan place deepening the struggle toward stability.

My point is that we do not know anyone else's story or the nightmare of the situations they are facing—situations that threaten to destroy all their forward momentum. God used this DMV situation to remind me of that and of my responsibility to show compassion to others.

Put on then, as God's chosen ones, holy and beloved, compassionate hearts, kindness, humility, meekness, and patience.

—Colossians 3:12

My call as a believer is not to fix anyone but to be compassionate, especially because I do not know the depths of someone's challenges or what the Lord is doing in their heart. The second thing God did for me through this experience is to remind me where He has brought me from, and who I am in Christ.

- I am a new creature (2 Corinthians 5:17).
- I am a child of God (John 1:12).
- I am accepted (Romans 15:7).
- I am a friend of Jesus (John 15:15).
- I have been justified and redeemed (Romans 3:24).
- I am not condemned no matter what the world says (Romans 8:1).
- I am set free from sin and death (Romans 8:2).
- I am God's workmanship created to produce good works for Him (Ephesians 2:10).
- I am no longer a slave, have been set free, and am an heir of the Most High God (Galatians 4:7; 5:1).
- I am chosen, holy, and blameless before God (Ephesians 1:4).
- I am alive with Christ because of God's mercy and love (Ephesians 2:4–5).
- I am light in the Lord where I was once darkness (Ephesians 5:8).
- I am a citizen of heaven (Philippians 3:20).
- I am complete in Christ (Colossians 2:10).
- I have been chosen of God, and I am holy and beloved (Colossians 3:12).
- God loves me (1 Thessalonians 1:4).

And as you read this, know that He loves you too. There is no mountain so high that He can't help you overcome it. There is no situation so difficult that resting in Him won't help. If you have not trusted Jesus, give Him a chance. Where man will let you down, He will never drop you.

For a moment after I received that letter, I thought about all the good stuff God has provided in my life, and I thought I would lose it all. I thought that my past was bigger than my present and that somehow my sins would overpower God. How foolish. I am grateful that doubt only lasted a moment before I came to my senses.

Did I commit the crimes of which I was accused? Yes. Should I give Caesar what I owed him? Absolutely. But to think that my issues are bigger than a God who has proven He loves me over and over again. No way. I serve the same God who helped David slay a giant and raised people from the dead. Frankly, He raised me from the dead, and He will raise you too if you let Him. Try Him, I dare you.

Chapter 35

LARGE AND IN CHARGE

The few years since COVID-19 have been some of the most amazing years of my journey with Jesus. Certainly, they have not always been easy. At times they were the most stressful experiences of my life. God however used the world's problems to teach me more about his faithfulness and how to follow Him as a leader. In short, He taught me to get out of the way. He provided during the storm of the pandemic and kept us solvent during the financial crisis that gripped us as the world shut down. He took care of my family, friends, and me as we were separated by time and distance. He continues to sustain the ministry as He always has.

Because He is God and we are not, when the world opened up after COVID-19, Miracle Hill was in the most stable financial position that we have ever been in. For the first time in anyone's memory, we were not struggling daily to make ends meet, and we had enough "extra" to begin strengthening some of the programs God has built over the years.

We have been strategically committed to going deeper as a ministry instead of wider, in order to provide for our staff. I firmly believe that the better we care for the shepherds, the better they will care for the sheep. We have improved some of our salaries, added training opportunities, hired care staff for our staff, and worked to improve other benefits. We have raised the wage for our lowest paid positions by five dollars an hour and have tried to communicate to the staff that they are loved.

I am grateful that we have been able to do these things, but it should be obvious that each shift adds to the bottom line and requires the Lord to provide more to keep the lights on across the ministry.

In December of 2022 we missed our development goal by $200 thousand for the month. This was the first time we had been behind in over two years. In February of 2023 we missed our goal by $300 thousand. For the first time since early 2020, I was sitting up and paying attention. I did not panic; my Miracle Hill experiences have taught me that panic is fruitless. Instead, I talked and prayed with Miracle Hill's leadership and waited for an answer from the Lord.

Honestly, in the back of my mind, there was a needling seed of doubt. There were questions swirling and creating fear in my head. I knew to pray and seek, but Ryan likes to act and fix.

- What about the 600+ people in our facilities? What if we can't afford to keep them there?
- What about the nearly 300 staff members? How are we going to pay them?
- What are we going to do if this continues?
- Where do we cut from the budget to make ends meet?

While all these thoughts threatened and demanded an answer, I kept walking through each day doing what the Lord called me to do: Love others.

The next morning after realizing the huge financial shortage, I headed to the Spartanburg County Sheriff's annual prayer breakfast. Sheriff Chuck Wright is a man of God and not shy about his faith. Each year he holds this event and brings together pastors, ministry workers, and other believers to pray for first responders, the county, and the country. As is customary, he delivers a speech, maybe it would be better to call it a sermon. In it he very plainly reminded me of a biblical truth: "I read this thing called the Bible . . . We win in the end," he said.

Thank you, Sheriff Wright. You are correct, sir; we do win. This doesn't mean that life will be easy or that we will not have struggles, but what is a financial shortfall to the Creator of the universe? I simply need to seek, pray, and trust. God will work out the rest.

After the prayer breakfast, I hopped in my truck and started driving down the highway. I had been playing telephone tag with a faithful friend of the ministry before walking into the event and finally connected with him by telephone as I drove. He asked me how I was, and what was new across the ministry. I told him all the Lord had been up to lately, bragging on God's goodness and faithfulness. The man then asked me what needs we had. I told him about the shortfall. He was silent for a moment and then calmly said:

Ryan, thank you for sharing this with me. This is confirmation to my wife and me of what the Lord is telling us. We felt the Lord calling us to give and believed He was telling us to send in a check for $500 thousand for operations. The check is in the mail.

I nearly ran off the road. Can you believe that? Not only did God provide, but he provided the exact amount we needed. We have absolutely nothing to worry about with God's goodness. He takes care of our every need and doesn't need us in the equation. He needs us to be obedient and speak up when He asks us to, but the movements on the board of life are His.

A gift of $500 thousand is amazing to be sure. What is as amazing to me are the thousands upon thousands of gifts that come in over the course of a year. God uses every gift to accomplish His work in the ministry.

Each day there are people listening to the prick of the spirit and giving in obedience. Their sacrifice whether it be one, five, ten, or twenty dollars is unparalleled evidence of His constant care and attention to His ministry.

> *Do not lay up for yourselves treasures on earth, where moth and rust destroy and where thieves break in and steal, but lay up for yourselves treasures in heaven, where neither moth nor rust destroys and where thieves do not break in and steal. For where your treasure is, there your heart will be also.*
>
> —Matthew 6:19–21

He has used so many people over the years to accomplish His goals at Miracle Hill. How dare I doubt His faithfulness. Thousands give of their treasure with a cheerful heart so that the least of these can be cared for today. God uses us all, regardless of the size of our wealth, to accomplish His purpose. Those who have more give more, those who have less, give as the Lord requires. Sometimes, like the widow's mite story in the Gospel of Luke, they give until it hurts.

As I sit here and type this, we are in another lean season. The cash flow coming in is less than the cash flow going out. Today, I am going to do my best to trust Him in this moment. He has always had control. The best thing that you and I can do is recognize our place in His story in our life. He is, whether we acknowledge it or not, large and in charge.

Chapter 36

CONCLUSION

We end this story where we started with three little letters on a page: God. If you remember back to the beginning of the story about my mother's illness, I said that this is where God had started His story in my life, but I didn't share how.

The year before my mother's accident, I had started having nightmares every night. Each night I would wake in the early hours of the morning and run into the safety of my mother's bedroom and arms. This happened night after night after night.

The morning that I found my mother was no different, and that is the only reason I was in her bedroom to find her in her medically compromised state. The day after that, I stopped having nightmares. I cannot explain why they stopped. For sure, I had a much greater reason to have them after that day, but I didn't. I do not think that God gave me nightmares, but He certainly allowed them. I also know that they disappeared after that day for no reason at all . . . but God.

I don't know how He was a part of that equation. I could ask Him when I get to Heaven, but I probably won't care once I get there. Years later when Mom passed away, long before I was a believer, my brothers divided up her earthly belongings. My brother Scott wound up with her

Bible, which was crammed with notes on the pages. As her mind and body betrayed her, she found an anchor in His word. No matter how confused she was, God was with her.

The same is true for us. No matter how confusing this world gets or how brightly it shines, Christ shines through the chaos, illuminating a path through relationship with Him. The Lord was with me when my life shifted on its axis, and He was with her. I didn't recognize the gravity of this until I wrote this book.

Years into sobriety, I came upon a conclusion about my life: "Praise God for my addiction." I don't think God caused my addiction. Nor do I think He is the author of the destruction of my past. He didn't create the chaos of my life, but He used it to show me the depth of my own depravity as well as the God-shaped hole at the center of myself. Jesus was with me through all of it, and every breath I take today is because of Him.

I don't know what your interpretation or definition of God was when we started this journey together, and it really doesn't matter. Look at the sum total of my life and tell me He is not real. Tell me He is not a personal God who wants nothing more than to walk with you through your life if you let Him. He has proven Himself time and time again as the Prince of Peace of my life.

> *For to us a child is born, to us a son is given; and the government shall be upon his shoulder, and his name shall be called Wonderful Counselor, Mighty God, Everlasting Father, Prince of Peace.*
> —Isaiah 9:6

This passage in the book of Isaiah was written over 2700 years from where we are today. God promised through this Old Testament prophet that He would send us a solution to our human issues. God knew what a struggle we would experience outside of relationship with Him. Seven hundred years after Isaiah penned these words, God, ever faithful to His promises, sent Jesus.

Jesus is the solution. Through Christ we find what we are looking for and an answer to that God-shaped hole in our life. Like Solomon, I chased the world and found it empty. Like so many of us, I looked for peace under every rock. I fulfilled the desires of my flesh and gained nothing. I found all roads led to emptiness and death. They promised me peace, but all they produced was fool's gold, a true counterfeit currency.

But God.

Trusting Jesus is the only avenue to peace that has ever existed in my life. He is the only pathway to peace for all of us. I understand that giving Him a chance to work a miracle in your life takes risk. I am so grateful that I did. It changed everything about my life. You too can change. Whether you are at the bottom of a bottle or the front row at church every Sunday, God will shift your life if you let Him. No matter how great or how insignificant our sin seems, God wants to wash it clean as snow. He wants you. All of you. Because He loves you.

But how can you hear the voice of God in your own life?

Now the boy Samuel was ministering to the LORD in the presence of Eli. And the word of the LORD was rare in those days; there was no frequent vision.

At that time Eli, whose eyesight had begun to grow dim so that he could not see, was lying down in his own place. The lamp of God had not yet gone out, and Samuel was lying down in the temple of the LORD, where the ark of God was.

Then the LORD called Samuel, and he said, "Here I am!" and ran to Eli and said, "Here I am, for you called me." But he said, "I did not call; lie down again." So he went and lay down.

And the Lord *called again, "Samuel!" and Samuel arose and went to Eli and said, "Here I am, for you called me." But he said, "I did not call, my son; lie down again." Now Samuel did not yet know the* Lord, *and the word of the* Lord *had not yet been revealed to him.*

—1 Samuel 3:1–7

God was clearly calling Samuel in the night. Samuel heard Him calling, but he was unfamiliar with His voice. This created confusion for the boy, but there are a few amazing lessons we can learn from Samuel.

Number one is the obvious answer; Samuel was listening. His ears were opened and ready to listen. He didn't have so many competing voices that he couldn't hear the One calling him.

Number two, Samuel was in a good position to listen. I mean he was lying down beside the Ark of the Covenant. He was as close to God as He could get.

Last, he had people around him to help him in his confusion. God used Eli to help Samuel discern that the Lord was beckoning him.

And the Lord *called Samuel again the third time. And he arose and went to Eli and said, "Here I am, for you called me." Then Eli perceived that the* Lord *was calling the boy. Therefore Eli said to Samuel, "Go, lie down, and if he calls you, you shall say, 'Speak,* Lord, *for your servant hears.'" So Samuel went and lay down in his place.*

And the Lord *came and stood, calling as at other times, "Samuel! Samuel!" And Samuel said, "Speak, for your servant hears."*

—1Samuel 3:8–10

The rest is history. Samuel was listening and present. He was open to God's movement in his life and God led him to be a great prophet.

- Are you listening?
- Are you being quiet enough that God can get your attention?
- Do you have people in your life who can guide you and help you discern God's will in your life?

There is no power so great that it can overcome the love of God. God is good, in all and through all. His love permeates the darkness and shines through our shame and guilt. It sets fire to the lies in our life, and if we will let Him in, He will show us those truths personally. He brings the only peace that can withstand the struggles of the flesh, trials of the world, and wiles of the devil. If you don't take anything else from this book except that, then I have done what I set out to do.

So that Christ may dwell in your hearts through faith—that you, being rooted and grounded in love, may have strength to comprehend with all the saints what is the breadth and length and height and depth, and to know the love of Christ that surpasses knowledge, that you may be filled with all the fullness of God.

Now to him who is able to do far more abundantly than all that we ask or think, according to the power at work within us, to him be glory in the church and in Christ Jesus throughout all generations, forever and ever. Amen.
—Ephesians 3:17–21

I am so grateful that I still get to call Miracle Hill home. Every day I am surrounded by amazing men and women who want to do the same thing I want to do, chase Jesus.

A new commandment I give to you, that you love one another: just as I have loved you, you also are to love one another.

—John 13:34

These warriors of the faith understand that true peace is found only in relationship with the Prince of Peace, so they scream it from the mountaintops. They delight in loving others in Jesus's name. Whether they are working in a shelter, loving a foster family, or picking up donations in a truck, they are loving the world like Jesus and for Jesus.

If you are already a Miracle Hill supporter, volunteer, and friend, thank you. If you don't know anything about the ministry and want to learn more, please reach out. You can find us on our website at www. miraclehill.org.

If you need help, do not have a friend in the world, and don't know where to turn, reach out to us. We are here and want to be your friend.

More importantly, call out to Jesus. He is with you right now and is beckoning to you. He is an ever-present help in time of need. He is waiting for an opportunity to sit quietly with you to wipe away your tears. He wants to show you what real peace is. He wants to be your friend even more than I do.

The Lord your God is in your midst,
a mighty one who will save;
he will rejoice over you with gladness;
he will quiet you by his love;
he will exult over you with loud singing.
—Zephaniah 3:17

Epilogue

POEM

One of the passions I found when I got clean was a deep love of poetry. I have always been a reader, and regardless of where I was or am in life, you can usually find me with my face shoved in a book. As my head cleared from the alcohol and drugs, I began to remember how much I loved writing and specifically how much I loved writing and reading poetry. In each written verse, poets articulate the truths of the heart that we stumble across with our words in everyday life.

This love for poetry started in the seventh grade when I was given an assignment to write a poem for class. Because I was already distracted with other pursuits in life, I did what was normal at the time, and I just didn't do the assignment. On the break before I entered class the day the assignment was due, I jotted down a one-page poem about hatred. I think I was mad at the time for having to do the assignment and so, I wrote about what was going on in my head. A few days later the teacher placed the winning poems on a cork board outside of her classroom and there was my poem for all the world to see. I wish I knew that teacher's name and could ask her why she chose my poem. I do not know what she saw in that scribbled note, but I believe because of that moment, I gained a belief that I could communicate my thoughts and feelings on paper if needed.

Over the years, I usually have a notebook of scribbled doodles and poems laying around somewhere. I have used poetry to woo women and to deal with my pain. As my head cleared of the drugs when I met Jesus, my mind filled with emotions, and I needed an outlet for dealing with life as I was experiencing it. I remembered poetry and fell back in love with it.

About a year later I was asked to give a testimony at the Oliver Gospel Mission in Columbia, South Carolina. While riding on a Greyhound bus that day, I wrote a long poem about my life and Jesus.

Five years later and a lifetime of decisions later, I was visiting a new church one Sunday evening when the pastor announced that the Sunday evening service would be different and would be an opportunity to share what the Lord has done and is doing in people's lives. The mic was open to the congregation, and anyone who wanted could share. I do not know what compelled me to do it, but I recited the poem again. Rocky Creek became my home church, and all these years later I still get jokes from the seniors at my church who remember that moment.

Below is that poem, now over twenty years old. At this point in my journey, I can identify some theological issues in it, but I haven't changed a single word except the number of years I have known Jesus. It is not a particularly good poem and doesn't use traditional rhyme and meter. It is meant as spoken word, but it is mine, and it summarizes my journey.

If you do not have an outlet to deal with your thoughts, feelings, experiences, and wounds, you need one. Journal, do art, write a poem, do something. On top of that, it should be clear that I deeply believe that we are meant to live in community, so find someone to talk to—a friend, a counselor, a pastor, someone. Deal with your garbage so that everyone else doesn't have to deal with its stench. If you don't know who to call, call me. I am easy to find.

Thank you for reading the story of God's grace in my life. Enjoy.

Somewhere Along the Way

Have you ever seen the inside of an empty darkened house?
It's shelves bare
no stockings hung by the chimney with care
Shadows of what was and once there held silently in the air
Dusty imprints of pictures long ago hung on my wall yet or no longer
there
I lost these things somewhere along the way

My house that was once filled with laughter and giggles
Now echoes against bare walls
The only remnants of life litter the ground around me
As empty 40s of OE or mirrors stained with cooked 8-balls
My heart slams with thoughts of lost rocks and dirty needles
Cockroaches and dead beetles

I stare at this
Thinking of my next fix
My drugs I tend to mix
You take one
I might take six
Or think of how many licks it takes to get to the center of this problem

I think my mom and my dad
Scared in the middle of the night of the night
I ran in their room
Cradled in love that no bogeyman can penetrate
Or birthday candles I blew out when I still believed in wishes
I lost these things somewhere along the way

Until I came to a place where my own father not didn't but wouldn't
recognize my face
My mother she passed
As candles burning brightly on cakes tend to do
I missed out on her
I lost her somewhere along the way

My brothers, they married
Nieces and nephews were born, but not introduced to me
For I was too scary
So I gripped back at my bottle
Until I could just barely,
Just barely
Watch my family go
merrily merrily merrily merrily
My life was but a dream

Days they passed
Melting in and out of each other
As interchangeable parts
Of the same psychotic puzzle
I should have been trapped in a cage
Tied down and muzzled
Instead of spitting game on the street

Were you homeless?
Oh for sure
I lost it all
Everything that I had
The whole kit and kaboodle
Somewhere along the way

Until one day
Indistinguishable from the others,
I was on a beach,
Drinking scotch and thinking of past lovers
And suicidal tendencies
I was just about ready to die
And that's when it happened.
I heard my Savior cry
Out me through the wind and the rain
Through all the garbage I have trapped in my brain,
And that's when those days that all look the same
Stop as I did dead in my tracks

As I stopped
Standing there in the sand,
I asked myself is there more than this man,
And a voice said, of course, all you have to do is try
And I fell down to my knees,
And I started to cry
As the blood in my tears burned at my eyes
Who can help me
He said, none other than I

So this is where I stood
With the wind at my back
My pockets filled with dread I realized there was no going back
See I was haunted
By the things I lost somewhere along the way

In John 3:16.
It states how God saves the one's whose lives are filled with strife
See for God so loved the world

That he gave his only begotten Son
That whosoever believes in Him
Shall not perish,
But have everlasting life

That was the beginning
This is the end
It's been ~~nearly~~ ~~1~~20 plus years since I found my new friend
You might want to know how far I've come from
Second Corinthians states that I'm a new creation
the old is gone and the new has come.

No more drugs
No more lies
No more unwanted goodbyes
Or overdosed highs from overcooked heroin pies
I lost these things somewhere along the way

God has unchained me
See he's setting me free
And I can do all things
Like in Philippians 4:13
I can do all things in Christ,
who strengthens me

Some same man that sounds good
I want to stop this insane ride and get out of the hood
Others scream at me at the top of their lungs with the same blood filled
eyes
I can't get out of this ever-changing maze
I can't stop getting high
Or getting hurt

Or hurting the ones that I love
Your story Ryan it fits me like a glove
See we've all lost things somewhere along the way

Maybe a wife
Or the smile from our kids as they played in the yard
I'm not saying it's easy
Man I know that it's hard
What you gotta do is let Christ play your cards

You might say not for me
I can't let go of this hand
Let me tell you
I am letting Christ play mine man
And since He's sat at the table
I know I've got nothing to lose
Nothing to hide
I don't have to commit crimes
Or do time
Man, I feel fine

So, what do you think I've lost somewhere along the way
In Christ
I've lost nothing

—Ryan T. Duerk 9.29.23

Miracle Hill Ministries Informational Page

Miracle Hill exists that homeless children and adults receive food and shelter with compassion, hear the Good News of Jesus Christ, and move toward healthy relationships and stability.

Miracle Hill Ministries is a nonprofit organization in the Upstate of South Carolina dedicated to providing extensive services to adults in the form of food, shelter, clothing, counseling, personal development, and addiction recovery. It is the largest provider of residential services to those experiencing homelessness in the Upstate of South Carolina with over 600 people in care on any given night. It also serves children who have been removed from their families through our foster home community, residential foster care program, and family ministry center.

If you want more information about the ministry, want to get involved, or are in need of help, please call us at (864) 268-4357, or use the QR code below.

www.ingramcontent.com/pod-product-compliance
Lightning Source LLC
Chambersburg PA
CBHW070529090426
42735CB00013B/2916